The Land of Fair Play

American Civics From A Christian Perspective

Christian Liberty Press

George Washington read Thomas Paine's inspiring words to his weary men on Christmas Eve, 1776, just before the battle of Trenton and the turning point of the Revolutionary War.

These are the times that try men's souls. The summer soldier and the sunshine patriot will, in this crisis, shrink from the service of their country; but he that stands it now, deserves the love and thanks of man and woman. Tyranny, like hell, is not easily conquered; yet we have this consolation with us, that the harder the conflict, the more glorious the triumph. What we obtain too cheap, we esteem too lightly; it is dearness only that gives every thing its value. Heaven knows how to put a proper price upon goods; and it would be strange indeed if so celestial an article as freedom should not be so highly rated.

ISBN 1–930092–98–9

Christian Liberty Press
502 W. Euclid Avenue
Arlington Heights, IL 60004

Copyright © 1994
1998 Printing

TABLE OF CONTENTS

BARON STEUBEN.   GOV. ARTHUR ST. CLAIR.   SECRETARY SAMUEL A. OTIS.   ROGER SHERMAN.   GOV. GEORGE CLINTON.
CHANCELLOR ROBERT R. LIVINGSTON.   GEORGE WASHINGTON.   JOHN ADAMS.   GEN'L HENRY KNOX.

WASHINGTON TAKING THE OATH AS PRESIDENT OF THE UNITED STATES,

APRIL 30, 1789

TO THE TEACHER

The urgent need for teaching the theory and practice of American government to our boys and girls at the earliest practical moment in their schooling is now widely recognized. Far too many young people in our nation's schools fail to complete their high school education. Therefore, to delay the formal teaching of civics until high school is to permit many of our boys and girls to grow up with no accurate knowledge of our governmental structure. In our new realization of the dependence of America upon the understanding and devotion of her every citizen, the desirability of ending this condition has become clear to every one.

Among the scores of works on American civics, there are almost none that attempt to describe the theory of our government and its essential machinery with the simplicity attempted here. The teaching of community civics in the lower grades has been well developed and a number of excellent volumes stressing the practical and local operations of government, street-cleaning, the fire department, and so on have been published. At the other end stands the many comprehensive, detailed, and technical textbooks, suited to mature high school or college use. It is for the field between that this volume has been designed as the result of much study, observation and consultation with teachers.

The plan of the book was the natural consequence of its aim. Since the theory, machinery and services of our national government formed the prime subject to be taught, it seemed essential to begin with this material. It is the opinion of many teachers that this method follows the natural interest of pupils and affords the clearer path. Certainly, the simplicity of the family and of local government is at least visible and sharply defined. With the aid of the playground analogy, the elements of our governmental theory can be made easily understandable by pupils in junior high or high school. Since a clear view of the organic relation of nation, State, and local government was a first essential, a logical chapter arrangement was followed in preference to an arrangement by lessons.

Of the questions for discussion, the most important are obviously the ones developing the State laws and local facts of government. The material for answering these questions (the form of ballot used in a State, local boundary-line, the names of local officials, etc.) is often not immediately accessible. But the value of these concrete examples is very great. The ideal system is, of course, for the members of the class to obtain the information from election officials, tax assessors, local members of the State Legislature, and others. The Secretary of State can be applied to at the State capital. One of the standard newspaper almanacs and the State year-book will often be of use. Time, of course, limits the amount of this local application of theory and law which a teacher can arrange; but it cannot be too strongly urged that the theory of government be as far as possible worked out in concrete laws, maps, ballots, and persons.

The text of the Constitution is included in the volume and frequently referred to in the belief that, only thus, can an appreciation of its basic importance be gained. No detailed analysis of the Constitution has been attempted. In the conception of the writer, it is the fundamental fact of its organic relationship to our citizenship duties that is chiefly important.

GEOFFREY PARSONS

ACKNOWLEDGMENTS

The publisher would like to thank Mr. Gary DeMar for giving us permission to use selections from his copyrighted text entitled *Ruler of the Nations* © 1987.

We also would like to thank Mr. Rus Walton, from Plymouth Rock Foundation, for permitting us to use four of their biographical sketches on the founding fathers.

> *The choice before us is plain, Christ or chaos, conviction or compromise, discipline or disintegration. I am rather tired of hearing about our rights and privileges as American citizens. The time is come, it now is, when we ought to hear about the duties and responsibilities of our citizenship. America's future depends upon her accepting and demonstrating God's government.*
>
> Peter Marshall

CREDITS

Author	**Mr. Geoffrey Parsons**
Revised and Edited by	**Mr. Edward J. Shewan**
	Mr. Lars R. Johnson
	Mr. Michael J. McHugh
Typesetter	**Lina Fetalco King**

First printing, 1994

Second printing, 1995

Third printing, 1996

CHAPTER 1

The Spirit of America

The Spirit of Fair Play - Every American boy and girl learns on the playground the true spirit of America, which is nothing else than fair play; fair play for every one, big and little, neither bullies nor cheats allowed. You can sum up the whole object of American Government by saying that it seeks to give every American, man or woman, boy or girl, rich or poor, an equal chance. Every boy and girl in America wishes to win, to succeed, to become great and famous. There is more ambition in America than any other country in the world. That is because every boy and girl has a better chance in America than in any other country in the world. Our country is far from perfect; we have our faults and injustices; as has every country. There are cheats and bullies in business as well as play. But we try to keep the game of life fair and we have succeeded by God's grace in making America the land of opportunity.

The poorest boy can become President. Ronald Reagan, who worked as a radio operator as a young man, lived to become a famous President. Every position, every success, stands open for each boy to try to win. Every girl can learn as much as she can and enter any business or work that appeals to her. Mr. Ray Kroc, who started out working as a soda fountain attendant in his uncle's drugstore in Chicago at the age of fourteen, eventually became the founder of the world famous McDonald's restaurant chain. He is but one of hundreds of Americans who have won their way to the highest success, because they had the freedom to pursue their dreams.

Now it is fair play, and only fair play, that makes this possible; that gives this chance to rich and poor alike. As in games, so in work we try our hardest to win, to succeed. But we play fair. We obey the rules. We give every boy and girl a fair start. We put bullies and cheats out of the game, and we aim to give every one an equal chance to succeed. That is the spirit of America. No one is a true American who does not try to live up to this standard of fairness.

There is no room for king or noble or any favored class in this free country. Every American is as good as his brains and character and manners, and no better.

*Five Reasons for America's Success

Today in our affluent society, we are enjoying so much of the fruits of this great system of ours that most of us forget just how and why we have become so prosperous. How is it that six percent of the world's population can produce almost one-half of the world's wealth? How could the American people in the short span of five generations, have changed an undeveloped wilderness continent into the tremendously rich and powerful nation that we now take for granted?

First, our founding fathers wrote the Constitution, the greatest document to govern people that the world has even seen. Living and working under our

Constitution and Bill of Rights, Americans created the most successful major society in all human history—and they did it all without government aid . . . .

It was built on these five principles:

1. We had a *belief in God*—and this religious background made us reliable and dependable with one another.
2. We had *limited government*—and this limited our national expenses and gave us surplus capital for tools and a good living standard.
3. We had *individual freedom*—every man could work at what he wanted.
4. We had *incentive*—which was simply the right to keep the fruits of our labor.
5. We had *competition*—the thing that makes businessman and employee alike serve his fellow man well.

The thinking of earlier leaders molded our American heritage. For example, Patrick Henry said, "If my family has freedom, and I have not given them one shilling, they would be rich. If they would not have freedom, and I have given them the whole world, they would be poor."

Thomas Jefferson put it more simply, "As government advances, freedom gives way." He was echoed much later by Woodrow Wilson—"Liberty has never come from government. The history of liberty is the history of limitation of governmental power, not the increase of it."

America became a place where the common man could be uncommon; where a man could become whatever his energy, his intellect, and his manhood could make him. This was the challenge, the hope, and the American heritage that touched and inspired hearts everywhere.

That freedom which our founding fathers gained for us is the cornerstone upon which this nation is built. We, in America, have been able to deliver in unbelievable abundance what Marxism, collectivism, Socialism, and fascism can only promise. But freedom rests, and always will, on *individual responsibility, courage,* and *faith.* It was exactly these qualities which have made the United States the most prosperous nation the world has ever known.

What truly concerns me is that for two centuries, because of the individual strength of each citizen, we guarded and nurtured our hard-won freedom. Gradually, though, as we have become more prosperous, we have also become less willing to shoulder individual responsibilities. More and more, we have government do what the individual should do. Either we will again assume the responsibility required by freedom or that light will go out in America. And if it does, it will go out all over the world. If the wealth, luxury and leisure that our system has brought us make us smug and complacent, willing to load our responsibilities on our government, we will lose—and deserve to lose—all these fruits of freedom.

*Five Reasons for America's Success, written by Walter Knott of Knott's Berry Farms.

Questions on the Text

1. What is the spirit of America?
2. What is the object of our government?
3. Why is there no nobility in America?
4. List five reasons why the United States is successful.

CHAPTER 2

The Captain, the Umpire, and the Rules

Captain and President – When a group of boys wish to start a ball team one of the first things they do is to choose a captain. No team can play well without a captain, and a good one. He decides where each boy shall play, directs the practice, makes out the batting list, and gives orders in a game - when to play up for a batter, when to change pitchers, and so on. He is the general of the forces in the field, and a good captain of a ball team is quite as important as a good general in a battle.

The President of the United States is the captain of the country. He does for the whole country very much the kind of things that your captain does for your baseball team. The country selects him to be their general, their leader. If we are good Americans we will select a godly and wise President. The President of the United States has a tremendous task and all sorts of things to do. It is a much more difficult thing to lead a nation of approximately 250,000,000 men, women, and children than to lead a team of nine ball players. But he is chosen by the people of the country much as you choose your baseball captain, and he leads the people much as your captain leads you.

Umpire and Judge – Next is the umpire. You can play a small game without an umpire, but there is likely to be trouble and dispute over close decisions, and no big game is ever played without an umpire. He belongs to neither team and is chosen to call balls, strikes, fouls, and outs fairly, without favoring either side.

Our judges are umpires chosen to make fair decisions in the matters of business and life. They are elected because they are fair-minded men, and fitted to hear both sides of a dispute and decide fairly which man has broken a law. If a player in a baseball game spikes a fielder intentionally, the umpire punishes him by putting him out of the game. Just the same, if a person knocks you down and steals your wallet or purse, the judge punishes him by sending him to jail.

Rules and Laws – This brings us to the question of rules, of laws. Have you ever seen the printed rules of baseball? They make up many pages of fine print. Most of them you know without thinking - how many strikes a batter is allowed, which way to run around the bases, and so on. But other rules, especially some of the newer changes, puzzle the most experienced players. The umpire is trained to know all the rules and to hold the players to them.

Now stop and think what a hopeless mess a game of baseball would be without rules that everyone had to follow. Each player would be doing as he pleased, a big boy who was a bully could stay at bat all day if he wished to, and a boy who wished to cheat could be as unfair as he cared to without any one to stop him. There would be no fair play for anybody.

It is rules and obedience to them that make fair play possible. The laws are nothing more than the rules of life, by which every honest man and woman is glad to live. Most of them every boy and girl knows and obeys without thinking, because they are the simple rules of right and wrong. It is a crime to steal; it is a crime to attack anyone. You can see that life would be a wild scramble without laws based upon the Bible and courts to enforce them. Thieves and cheats would have an open field, and fair play would be utterly impossible.

Freedom Through Laws – That is what American freedom means. It is not freedom to do exactly as we please, for that would produce anything but real freedom. It is freedom to do our utmost to succeed, provided we play fair as defined by God's law and the United States Constitution. As a matter of fact, no one who lives in the same city or county with other people can be entirely free to do what he wishes. Someone has said that "only a fish is wholly free," and that is about true. What America tries to do is give just as much freedom as possible and give it to every one alike. The result is that America is the freest country in the world, because its people are blessed with a constitutional form of government that recognizes the inalienable rights of citizens to enjoy God-given liberty.

Who makes the rules and laws of fair play? In baseball, it is men chosen by the big leagues who meet once a year. In our government, it is our lawmakers, or legislators, the Congress that meets every year at Washington; and these are chosen by the votes of every registered voter just as is the President.

The Three Branches of American Government – That is the main outline of our American Government, and you see how much its plan resembles the plan of a baseball game. You cannot have a successful baseball team without (1) a leader; you cannot play a baseball game peaceably and fairly without (2) an umpire; and you cannot possible play without (3) rules. That is the precise theory of our government. We call these three parts the executive, judicial, and the legislative branches of our federal government.

What Government Does – The rules of baseball relate to only one thing, a baseball game. Government touches our whole daily life, waking or sleeping. It also affects our business, health, safety, and happiness. It includes all those things that we can do best together: the building of roads; fire and police protection day and night; the delivery of mail; the coining of money; fighting a common enemy with military forces; and so forth. In a savage country, every man carries a club and is his own policeman. In a civilized country, all unite and hire a policeman to act for all. It is more convenient and more efficient. Government is the organization we use to do all these things in common. So, the reach of our government is very wide. This reality occasionally creates problems, for those in power sometimes forget where their power and authority came from – *the people*! When government agencies seek to rule without the consent of the governed, it is the right, it is the duty of every American to re-establish the limits of the government's authority through protest, court action, or the ballot box. The key to keeping the government fair is by each citizen diligently requiring that government operate within its limited sphere of authority.

Questions on the Text

1. What does the President do for us?
2. What do our judges do for us?
3. Why do we have laws?
4. Are Americans free to do whatever they wish?
5. Who makes our laws?
6. What are the three branches of American government?
7. Why do we have a government and what does it do?

Questions for Discussion

1. What makes a good captain in a game?
2. Do you know the names of any famous captains of ball teams?
3. Who were our Presidents during wars?
4. Can you state six rules from either baseball, football, basketball, or in any other team sport?
5. Have you a copy of a baseball guide containing the rules in full?
6. Can you state some of the penalties for breaking the rules in a baseball game?

CHAPTER 3

The Team

Constitutional Republic – All these are important: the captain, the umpire, and the rules. But you cannot play ball without a team. After all is said, it is the whole team that wins a game or loses it. It is the team that does the work.

Now in a well-run ball team, this is recognized and the team runs things. The captain is chosen by vote of all the players. The most important questions are put before the team for decision. The captain runs the team not to please himself or any one or two players, but for the whole nine. That is the American way. It is the democratic way. It is the way the American nation is governed.

Despotism – You all may have seen teams which were not run in this way - in which one big boy, something of a bully, got together with smaller boys and made them do as he wanted. The smaller boys lacked the spirit to stand up for their rights. Whether the captain thought he was doing the right thing for the team or not, the boys had to live with what the captain said. This is not the American way.

This is how a despot rules, with absolute power. Even when a despot thought he was being helpful, he still ruled without the consent of the people. In the past, many monarchs, like the Czars of Russia, or King Henry VIII, of England (1509-1547) governed in this way. Today, despots are more likely to be premiers, presidents, or generals than kings. President Saddam Hussein of Iraq is a good example of a modern despot. We usually call such despots, "dictators."

Anarchy – Suppose, on the other hand, you tried to run a team without any leader. Probably no boys were ever foolish enough to attempt this plan, but suppose some boys did. You can imagine what confusion and quarrelling there would be and how poor a game such a team would play. Every boy would do as he pleased and boss just as many other boys as he could. We saw how important rules and an umpire are. Take away the captain too, and you have exactly the condition known as anarchy, which means the attempt to run a country with no government whatever. Certain theorists, impressed by the defects of government, have urged anarchy as a solution to all our troubles. But, as you can see, the remedy would be far worse than the disease. We would have a whole nation of despots, every one ruling himself as he pleased and just as many of his friends and neighbors as he could. The mere fact that people are by their nature, sinful and corrupt, rules out the possibility of a successful government being operated on the premise of each person doing what he feels is right.

Oligarchy – Sometimes it is not one boy who runs a team but three or four boys. Perhaps they have more money than the others and can buy bats, balls, and masks, and therefore think they have the right to tell the others what to do. Perhaps they are older and bigger than the rest. Well, that is not American, either. When it comes to electing a captain or deciding any important matter, every player on the team ought to have his say. Big or little, rich or poor, they are all players; it is their team, and they ought to run it. That is the theory of America. It is government, of the people, by the people, and for the people.

When, instead, a few individuals put their ideas over the rest, you have what is called an oligarchy. The word means a government by the few. Occasionally a ruling class is the best, but usually they only think they are because they are the richest and the most powerful. Even if they happen to be the wisest and finest, it is un-American because our theory of government provides citizens with the power to remove leaders who fail to rule justly, without having to overthrow them by way of violent revolution. The communist government of the People's Republic of China is a contemporary example of an oligarchy.

One form of oligarchy is known as aristocracy, which means government by the best. An aristocracy is made up of a privileged minority (often called nobles or the nobility) who have usually inherited their positions of power and wealth. Members of the aristocracy generally rule a country along with a monarch. Few countries today have a very powerful aristocracy. An example of a powerful aristocracy is the Saudi family that rules in the Kingdom of Saudi Arabia.

England, America, and Germany – A typical aristocracy was England at the time of the American Revolution. George III was not a despot, because the nobility and upper classes of the country shared the power of governing with him. But the working people of England had nothing to say whatever in the government. Power belonged only to nobles and landowners. A limited monarchy is another name for such a government, since the power of the monarch or king is not absolute, but is limited by the power of others.

Do not make the mistake of thinking that the England of today is either a despotism or an aristocracy. It is a democratic monarchy and its government is almost as democratic as our own. It is a limited monarchy in which the limits have swallowed the monarch, whom simply is a figurehead to symbolize the unity of the nation and represent it on state occasions. The real head of England is the Prime Minister, who acts for the people of England just as our President acts for the American people.

That is the normal growth of governments, away from despotism, through limited monarchies to individual liberty. England has reached democracy in fact, but not in name. The federal or central government has much of the power of a despot. The people of Germany, like so many of the people of Europe, are governed by a type of democratic socialism. Such governments are quite similar to an aristocracy in that they contain a large and powerful central government and rule their people through bureaucratic and arbitrary regulations.

The People's Rule – In America, the only rulers are the people. As we have seen, they elect a President to lead them, legislatures to make new laws or rules for them, and judges to act as umpires for them when laws are disputed. But the

President, the legislatures, and the judges are simply the agents of the people to carry out the wishes of the people. The Constitution of the United States, the highest law of the land, begins with the words: "We, the people of the United States ... do ordain and establish this Constitution for the United States of America." When a criminal is arrested or punished, the order reads not in the name of the judge or the officer, but in the name of "the people."

"Of the people, by the people, for the people" was Abraham Lincoln's description of the American system of government, and it is the best description there is.

A Republic – America is a republic that contains democratic forms. It has democratic form because the people rule it. It is a republic because the people rule it through representatives. The other kind of popular rule is sometimes called a "pure democracy," and in it the people meet and run their government directly without electing any officers to act for them. This sort of democracy is possible only in a small community like ancient Athens or a modern New England town. But in America, we have joined together under the Constitution which clearly states the people rule through elected representatives. Therefore, the United States of America is not a "pure democracy," but rather a Constitutional Republic that contains certain democratic systems.

Questions on the Text

1. What is a democracy?
2. What is a despotism?
3. What is anarchy?
4. What is an oligarchy?
5. What is a limited monarchy?
6. What sort of government does England have?
7. What sort of government does Germany have at the end of twentieth century?
8. Who are the rulers in America?
9. What is a "pure democracy" and what is a republic?

Questions for Discussion

1. Can you name any other despots other than the Czars of Russia?
2. Can you name any limited monarchies?
3. How many republics can you name?
4. Are there any monarchies in the western hemisphere and republics in Asia?
5. What type of government currently exists in the People's Republic of China?

CHAPTER 4

Majority Rule

Government by Majority – Like most of the long words of government, majority rule is a thing which every American boy or girl is so familiar with, that it is taken as a matter of course. If there is a dispute in your team over anything, who should be captain, what team you will play next, where you will play, you all say what you want, and what the most of you want, that is what you all do. If eight vote one way and one the other, you all do as the eight wish. If seven vote one way and two the other, you all do as the seven wish. If six vote one way and three another, you all do as the six wish. If five vote one way and four another, you still, all nine of you, do as the five wish. Those who are outvoted swallow their ideas and do as the rest prefer. That is all there is to majority rule. (Majority comes from the Latin word *major* which means "great.")

I Won't Play – It is a simple idea, but it is at the bottom of all government by the people; and unless a people understand it and live by it, they cannot possibly run a successful government. You know how it is in a group of boys too young or too tough to play fair. In such a crowd, it is impossible to have a good baseball team or to play any game that is worth while. There is wrangling and fighting and sadness most of the time. "I won't play unless I can have my way" is the talk of the boy who is outvoted. Or if he is a bully, he puts up his fists and threatens to fight those who disagree with him.

There are certain young nations so unfitted for popular government that they behave exactly like these disorderly boys. Their people do not understand the first principle of majority rule. Every so often we read of a revolution in a Central American country, or some other part of the world. That simply means that the side which was outvoted at an election had seized the government by force of arms. No great issue of right and wrong was involved. The revolutionists simply refused to "play" unless they could run things. As you can imagine, there is no happiness, progress, or business success in a country thus given over to riot and bloodshed.

The Right of Revolution – There is one other point to remember. The time does come, once in a while, when it is not only necessary but one's sacred duty to resist a government. This has been called "the right of revolution," and our America was founded in just this way, as you have learned in your histories. Suppose in your crowd of boys the leaders tried to cheat you or steal from you. It would be your duty to resist and fight to the limit and break away altogether rather than submit. So in a nation, the government is sometimes tyrannical and unjust, and when all peaceable protest fails, a courageous and self-respecting people must and will fight as did our ancestors in the Revolution. The Second Amendment to our beloved Constitution, guaranteeing the people the right to keep and bear arms, was included in our national laws to secure the people's right of revolution against tyrants. Only tyrants fear an armed citizenry.

But in government, as in play, fighting must be a last resort, and no people are well-served to undertake armed resistance unless a vital question of right and justice is involved. The Declaration of Independence and the Bible both warn the American people not to engage in armed revolution over minor or petty problems with leaders in government.

The Dangers of Revolution – The American colonies were used to a large measure of self-government, and having declared their independence, quickly set up an orderly and secure rule. Aside from their war for freedom, there was little disturbance or bloodshed. Other revolutions have not been so fortunate. The French Revolution of 1789 lasted through many long and bloody years, while parties rose and fell and one popular tyrant succeeded another. The Russian Revolution went through the same bloody confusion. The Communist government originated as one of the most dangerous forms of despotism, rule by a class. Such a government is as much opposed to the American idea of rule by all the people as is despotism like that of the Czars of Russia.

Questions on the Text

1. What is majority rule?
2. When should we do what the majority wishes?
3. When have a people a right to revolt?
4. What are the dangers of revolution?

Questions for Discussion

1. How does a meeting find out on which side of a question the majority stands?
2. What reasons did our Declaration of Independence give for the Revolution?
3. What had the American colonists done to avoid a revolution (as set forth in the Declaration of Independence)?
4. What change in attitude would likely take place among government leaders if they knew that the people were disarmed and unable to effectively resist their acts of tyranny?

Right to Bear Arms

CHAPTER 5

The Laws of Freedom and Fair Play

American Liberty – Liberty is in the air we breathe in America. It is so much a part of our lives that we seldom think of it. We take it for granted, like the sky and a clear wind, and food and drink.

But those who came to America from the oppressed countries of Europe, especially from Russia after the Communist Revolution and the downfall of the Czar, and from Asia or other parts of the world, feel this liberty as something new and strange and wonderful. They feel that they are coming out of darkness into the light, from a house with low ceilings and narrow walls into the free and open air.

We should all strive to understand this liberty of ours–where it came from and how we can keep it. It is the most precious gift any American can obtain next to a personal relationship with Jesus Christ.

The Five Rights – There are five chief rights belonging to every American, old and young, that make American freedom what it is. They are:
1. Personal safety and freedom
2. Religious freedom
3. Free speech
4. Safety of property
5. Trial by jury

1. **Personal Safety and Freedom** – In a little town of Zabern in Germany, in 1913, a lieutenant, of noble birth, struck a lame cobbler with his sword because the poor man had laughed at him. There was a great to-do over the attack, but the Kaiser upheld the lieutenant, and he was never punished in any way. It was held that under German law he had done entirely right in hitting the lame cobbler.

That was a very brutal and outrageous case. But the same kind of interference with liberty happened constantly in Germany under its militarist rule. The German word *verboten* means forbidden, and every way that a German turned, to play or to work, he found something *verboten*. In his home, on the street, in business, he was surrounded by harsh rules and brutal army officers and nobles and royalty, to whom he was forced to give way. Nowhere was he a free man and safe from the harassment of arrogant bureaucrats.

Now, in America we can live as we please, safely and securely. Every man, woman, and child is protected from arrest and attack. We have no nobles and royalty to bow to. No officer of our army and navy would dream of slashing a civilian to make him respectful. The police are your servants, friends, and protectors. Our only rules are those necessary to punish wrong-doers, and to see that there is fair play, so that everybody has an equal chance to succeed.

An American home has a peculiar degree of protection. "A man's house is his castle" is the old English phrase, and this liberty, like many others, we inherited directly from our English forebears. The police cannot enter your home without a court order. An American home is a sacred spot that the law protects. The Fourth Amendment of the United States Constitution clearly acknowledges the right of each citizen "to be secure in their persons, houses, papers, and effects, against unreasonable searches and seizures."

2.   **Religious Freedom** – We can go to church where we will. That does not sound like anything extraordinary to an American. Of course we can go to church where we choose. But in many parts of the world there is no religious liberty at all. In the former Soviet Union, the Christians led an oppressed life because of their religious faith. They were abused, imprisoned, and killed by the hundreds and thousands. They were kept as prisoners in various concentration camps, along with other political prisoners. The camps were called gulags.

In America the Jew has his synagogue, the Buddhist his temple, and the Muslim his mosque. He is not only free to worship as he wills, but his worship is not hindered in any respect. He can aspire to any success or office. So it is with all of us, Protestant, Catholic, Jew, or any other person of faith. Most Americans have a strong religious faith, but they feel that religion is something each man must decide for himself. They do not dream of forcing anybody to believe as they do or of punishing anybody for a strange belief. The legacy of religious tolerance in America is a fruit of our nation's Christian heritage.

3.   **Free Speech** – Free speech is another precious part of American liberty. It means that Americans can meet whenever they want to talk over what they will. If they do not like their government, they can meet and say so. If they wish a law changed they can meet and say so. The freedom to state their views in writing is also included. That means that American newspapers, as well as, television and radio personalities can speak of anything they think is wrong and say why, and nobody can stop them. The only limit is you must say and print the truth. You must not misstate the facts. Lying is against the law for grown-ups just as much as for children.

Compare this with China. The Chinese newspapers could not print the truth about the incident in 1989 in which hundreds of college students were murdered at the order of government leaders who wished to punish them for seeking democratic reforms in Communist China. They had to print exactly what these leaders ordered them to print. The massacre of the students in Tiananmen Square was not told about at all in the Chinese papers. Throughout the weeks of protest and unrest, people were lied to and deceived in their newspapers by order of the government.

You can see how important free speech is to a nation wishing to be free and to be at liberty to manage one's own affairs, like our own Constitutional Republic. Unless public men can tell the truth and newspapers can print the truth, the people cannot know what is going on, whom to trust, and how to vote. The control of speech, radio and television, and newspapers and books is one of the bulwarks of tyrannical governments. Free speech is the beginning of all free government, for only in such a country can citizens be free to print and read the Holy Bible, which is the only truth that can set a people free.

4.   Safety of Property – Property is anything you own - a postage-stamp, a bicycle, a gun, a video camera, or a house and lot. The right to own things, to have them for your very own so that nobody can take them away, is very important. Unless a man can keep what he earns and buys with his savings, he can never get ahead in the world; and he will always be dependent upon some rich man for charity. He can never be free. In old Russia, almost all the land was owned by a few great nobles and rich men; and these took good care that the Russian peasants should not own any land or much of any property. Thus, the peasants of old Russia were little more than slaves.

In the Middle Ages throughout Europe, kings and nobles helped themselves to taxes very much as they desired. The peasants and tradesmen and artisans were obliged to give up a huge slice of their earnings and property to their overlord. That was the feudal system, and the history of democracy is the history of how the people slowly got the better of their kings and nobles and gained the right to hold their property undisturbed.

In America, what a man earns is his own and no one can take it away from him. With it he can buy whatever he chooses, a house, land, anything. He must pay taxes, but they must be fair and reasonable. If his land is needed for some public improvement of benefit to every one, such as a railroad or a school, the State can take it, but must pay full value for it. We might properly call this right to own property, without interference from any one, the right to pursue happiness.

5.   Trial by Jury – In past centuries, despotic kings ran the courts as they pleased and sent anybody to prison or beheaded anybody they wished. Slowly the people have won fair and impartial trials. Trial by jury, that is, trial by twelve of his neighbors, is the right of every American when he is accused of a serious crime. No judge can convict him, no police officer, no politician, no rich and powerful man. Plain American citizens, like himself, alone can send him to jail.

Moreover, the trial must be public. Secret trials have always been the favorite weapon of a despot. "Star Chamber proceedings" was a common expression for any secret decision by any group of people. It dates back to 1487 in England, when Henry VII founded a special court that sat in secret, tortured prisoners, and condemned them without a hearing. It is said to have sat in a room with gold stars on the ceiling and thus was named the Star Chamber. It was abolished in 1641.

Also the prisoner cannot be compelled to testify against himself. Other features of American justice will be described later. You can see how important a part of American fair play is "trial by jury," with all it signifies. The jury system also provides an important check on legislative tyranny by giving ordinary citizens the right and opportunity to refuse to enforce statute laws that they are convinced are immoral, unconstitutional, or unjust.

Sources of Our Liberty – These rights of American liberty did not come into being suddenly. They were the outgrowth of five centuries of struggle in England against tyranny. Our Revolution freed the colonies from unjust rule by an English king and gave them the chance to develop as a great, free nation. But the foundations of personal liberty had already been laid in England. Later on in this text, we shall see that even our new form of government was not a wholly strange and untried invention, but was the natural outgrowth of all the experience of the past. There, indeed, was the greatest feat of our forefathers; the ability that saved them from the wreck and ruin that have followed in the wake of most revolutions. They had the courage to fight to the death for freedom; and they also had the common sense to know that freedom by itself, without wise laws to control it and insure fair play, is nothing; and that wise laws cannot be invented overnight, but must come as people study and apply Biblical principles.

Magna Carta and Bill of Rights – These are the two great landmarks in the English struggle for personal liberty, and every American lives under their safeguards, for their provisions were brought over by the colonists and written into the law of our land. Magna Carta, or the Great Charter, was signed by King John at Runnymede, near London, in 1215. He had been tyrannical and cruel until the nation could stand his oppression no longer. So the strong men of England drew up this statement of their rights and compelled the king to sign it. It is the foundation and beginning of our liberty. The right to a prompt and fair trial, the right to trial by jury, the forbidding of taxation except as imposed by the people's representatives, and the right to local self-government are among the great rights which it declared.

However, the battle was not over and tyrannical kings repeatedly broke the rules laid down by Magna Carta. Finally, in 1689, when William III was made king, the Bill of Rights was drawn up. Free speech, the right to bear arms, and a number of other important rights were added to the common privileges of every Englishman by this great document.

King John of England was forced to sign the Magna Carta in 1215. This "great charter" said that the "law is greater than the King." The important principle of rule by law through a covenant that mutually binds leaders and common people alike, was also included within our U. S. Constitution. This principle is often stated as "Freedom *through* laws."

Religious liberty had not been won at this time in England, and it was religious persecution that drove many of the colonists to seek their fortune in America. There was persecution in many of the colonies, and complete religious freedom was gained only after a long struggle.

Civil and Political Rights – The rights we have been describing are often called civil rights, the word "civil" here meaning common to all members of a nation. They are contrasted with political rights, that is, the right to share in the government, to vote, and to hold office. Our forefathers found that the best way to protect their civil rights (that is, the rights of personal liberty we have described) was to gain political rights. So they insisted upon the right to vote, and that is how our American theory developed—government should be run not by a few people or any class, but by all people. However, the distinction still remains. All Americans, men, women, boys and girls, have civil rights simply because they are Americans; but only certain Americans have the "elective franchise," that is, the privilege of voting. The people determined who should be qualified to vote. No one under eighteen, for instance, is permitted to vote; but every boy and girl has exactly the same rights of personal liberty as any grown man or woman.

Questions on the Text

1. What are the five chief rights of every American?
2. Explain what each of them means.
3. Why is free speech essential in a Constitutional Republic like our own government?
4. What is property and why is its safety important to all of us?
5. What are some of the safeguards that American justice throws about an accused person?
6. What were the sources of American liberty and how many centuries of struggle does it represent?
7. When was Magna Carta signed and what rights did it establish?
8. When was the Bill of Rights enacted and what rights did it establish?
9. When was religious liberty established in America?
10. Distinguish between civil and political rights and give an example of each.

Questions for Discussion

1. Can you think of anything that your city or village does to make your life safe?
2. What were the religious persecutions in America before the Revolution?
3. What is a massacre?
4. Is there any mention of God or religion in the Constitution?
5. Why is the jury system so important to personal liberty?

Test 1

CHAPTER 6

The Constitution

The Constitution – We saw that the object of all laws, and the reason we have judges to say what they mean is to secure freedom and fair play, just as the rules and the umpire secure fair play in a ball game. But these great rights of freedom we have just described have a special importance. They are the foundation upon which all other rights rest. With them our freedom is secure. Without them, without any one of them, our whole system of liberty and fair play might crash to the ground. Therefore, special safeguards have been thrown about them. They have been set apart in a vital document, called the Constitution, to stand, like the Ten Commandments, above all other law. The general plan of our government forms part of the Constitution. These rights of the people form the rest. Every American boy and girl should understand exactly how the Constitution works, how it is protected, and what it does for each of us.

Its Safeguards – Any ordinary law can be changed at any time by Congress without much delay. But the Constitution is different. It can be changed only after long discussion and by the overwhelming vote of the people. A bare majority of legislators can pass a law in Congress. It takes the vote of two-thirds of the House and Senate to offer an amendment (that is, a change) to the Constitution; and after the amendment has passed Congress; it must be approved by three-fourths of the States, that is, 38 out of 50. This procedure insures long discussion and makes certain that no change can be made in the Constitution unless the country is overwhelmingly for it.

The Two Reasons – There are two reasons for these safeguards thrown about the Constitution. One is that the Constitution holds the thought of our wisest and noblest men, from Washington down. We must not lightly change what they have wrought. There must be thorough debate by every one and general agreement before we act. There must be appeal to second thoughts, which are often the best. There must be no hasty tinkering with so solemn a document, the guardian of our lives and liberties. (A Constitution is, in essence, a contract that clarifies the relationship between a people and their government.)

The second reason goes back to what has been said about majorities and tyranny and the right of revolution. America is the oldest republic on a large scale in the world. It has weathered every storm, very largely because our Constitution prevents evil acts by majorities. The Constitution is binding not only on you and me, but upon Congress as well. Our legislators cannot pass a law taking away any of the rights and liberties protected by the Constitution. Or, rather, they can pass such a law, but as soon as the Supreme Court of the United Sates decides that the law attempts to do what the Constitution forbids, the law is wiped out. That is what "unconstitutional" means. That is the great service that our Supreme Court of the United States, the most powerful court in the world, does for each of us. This plan of a Constitution binding upon everyone, with a court to enforce it, was an American invention. We can all be proud and thankful that our forefathers had the mind and skill to create this new and wise system. There is no other country in the world where personal rights are held so sacred or so carefully protected by the laws. No mere majority can ever take away our liberties or our rights without breaking the Supreme Law of the Land.

The Supreme Law – You can see why the Constitution is called the supreme law of the land. It stands above all other laws and above all our officers of government: Presidents, judges, legislators, policemen, every one. It is the faithful, tireless protector of every American. God alone can give rights to individuals. However, because men are sinful, citizens need the protection of godly laws to help secure their freedom from those leaders who would seek to play God. Our beloved Constitution is designed to limit the power of sinful men so they cannot destroy the God-given liberties of the people.

Questions on the Text

1. What is a Constitution?
2. What does our Constitution contain?
3. How can it be amended?
4. Upon whom is it binding?
5. What are the two reasons for the safeguards thrown about our Constitution?
6. When is a law unconstitutional?
7. Has it then any force?

Questions for Discussion

1. Have any of your school organizations constitutions?
2. How can they be changed?
3. How do by-laws differ from the rest of a club's constitution and why are they usually made easier to change?
4. How many amendments to the Constitution have been adopted altogether and what was the last one adopted?

CLOSED BY
ORDER OF
THE STATE

CHAPTER 7

The Duties of an American

Our Six Duties – America gives her citizens more opportunities than any country in the world, and she expects more from them. That is a general rule of life. You cannot get something for nothing in this world, either in government or anything else. The Scriptures exhort us to honor all men, especially those in authority over us. The Apostle Paul instructed Titus to remind the people "to be subject to rulers and authorities" (Titus 3:1). Therefore, it is not only a privilege as citizens, but it is our God-given responsibility to actively participate in these citizenship duties (Romans 13:1-7, 1 Peter 2:13-17). The six great things that every American must do for his or her country are:
1. Vote
2. Pay legitimate taxes
3. Do jury duty
4. Fight
5. Obey the laws
6. Pray

1.   The Vote – The first duty of every American, eighteen and older, is to vote. The actual voting takes only a few minutes on Election Day, which comes the first Tuesday after the first Monday in November. However, the duty is much more than simply voting. You must vote wisely, and that means you must read several different newspapers and keep track of what is going on. You must discuss it all with your friends and neighbors, you must attend political meetings and hear the candidates (that is, those running for office) tell what they intend to do. It takes a keen, wide-awake mind, that can read and inquire about the important issues of the day, to vote intelligently.

Moreover, voting is more than just the few minutes' work once a year. In order to vote you must first register, which means going on a certain day and putting your name down on the voting list. (This is to prevent fraud at the election.) Also you ought to vote at the primaries, the party elections, held some time before Election Day, at which the candidates of the parties are chosen. Also, there are other elections than the main one in November at which you ought to vote. If you live in a city or town, there is a municipal election. In addition, there is, in many cases a special local election which selects the public school board. All these elections will be described in more detail later. The point now to remember is that a good American citizen takes a constant interest in his government, follows all the elections carefully, and votes honestly and as wisely as he knows how at each election. No republic can be a success unless its voters help in this fashion by conscientious, wise voting.

2.   Taxes – A tax is similar to a collection or offering in church - or the sum you pay when every member of your team chips in to buy a new ball or bat. It costs a great deal to run our system of government. Your President, your judges, your legislators, your firemen, your policemen, must be paid salaries. Your army, navy, air force, and coast guard must be paid for. Your streets must be paved, your sewers maintained, your parks run. All this runs up to a tremendous sum, as you can imagine. But it is divided among everybody, and nobody has to pay a very large sum except for the very rich.

Taxes are not easy or pleasant to pay. In war time, when there is a great army to feed and equip and a great navy to build and supply, taxes are a heavy burden. But every loyal American pays his share fairly and gladly, for he knows that without an army and navy we should be conquered and lose all the blessings we cherish. God has established these authorities, and to rebel against them is an act of rebellion against what God has instituted. So Paul declares "This is also why you pay taxes, for the authorities are God's servants, who give their full time to governing. Give everyone what you owe him: If you owe taxes, pay taxes; if revenue, then revenue" (Romans 13:6-7).

The question arises, though, are Christians bound to obey every law, statute, and ordinance? Or pay every tax, excise, and duty? Most have never been confronted with such questions as: What must I do when man's law is contrary to God's law? Can I honestly pay a tax that I know is going to be used by the government for the aborting of an unborn child? Whom do I obey? What does God demand?

Many would simply say that Romans 13:1-2 teaches "blanket submission" to the civil government. Anytime the government wants to legislate ungodly laws, we are told that we must obey them because of Romans 13. But the author of the book of Romans is the same person who was in prison on numerous occasions for violating the edicts and laws of political leaders. There are many other examples in the Scripture where God's people refused to obey ungodly laws: the Hebrew midwives disavowed to kill baby boys, because they feared God more than Pharaoh; Rahab not only lied to her king, but hid spies and helped them to escape; Shadrach, Meshach and Abednego rebelled against Nebuchadnezzar by not prostrating themselves before the graven image; and Daniel, who had a high position in government, was thrown into the lion's den for disobeying King Darius' decree of praying only to government approved gods.

The New Testament also bears out the same principle that Peter so eloquently proclaimed, "We ought to obey God rather than men" (Acts 5:29). As citizens of this great land of fair play, we should obey our local, State, and national laws as long as they do not conflict with the Word of God. Our civil representatives have no legitimate authority to legislate any laws that will conflict with the Bible or the Constitution. Our civil government leaders must swear an oath to be subject to the Law of the Land. Civil leaders are, therefore, not a law unto themselves. Therefore, we should use our power and influence to help ensure that even the taxes that are mandated at the federal, State, and local level, are in keeping with the Bible. Ultimately the person who refuses to pay his tax must be sure that the tax is clearly unbiblical and not merely inconvenient.

3.   **Jury Duty** – We saw that trial by jury was one of the great blessings of American liberty. Now you cannot have juries without men and women to serve on

them. Therefore, every American must take his turn when the court summons the person to act as a juror. It means the loss of some time from a person's business or job, but that is part of the price we gladly pay for the benefit of safe, fair and humane trials.

4.   Fighting – The duty of every American to fight for his country when she is in peril is as old as the nation. Our country, with all its wonderful liberties, was born of heroic fighting. Without the glorious courage of the Revolution, the years of hard, bitter fighting against heavy odds, there would be no America today. In 1812, the nation was preserved from destruction by the sword. In 1917 and 1941, we entered the First and Second World Wars to make the world safe for democracy. The German threats of conquest were aimed not only against Belgium, France, Russia, and England, but against the United States and every other free people. We had to fight for our liberties, and for the liberties of the oppressed people. Conscription, the call of every fighting man to the colors, was a magnificent success in America because this duty of the citizen was universally felt. There was practically no opposition, no holding back. All America went to war gladly to defend those liberties which are more precious than life itself. In recent years, the United States has established an all volunteer army of fighting men. This concept of volunteerism, versus a mandated system of drafting new soldiers, has worked very successfully. The recent war in the Persian Gulf was fought with an all volunteer army and our troops were successful.

5.   Obey the Laws – Boys and girls with the right idea of sport and fair play do not try to cheat their opponents. Whether the umpire is looking or not, they play fair. They feel that it is dishonorable to win by cheating. As a matter of fact, a game played by cheats is about as unpleasant as a game can be. In cases where an umpire cannot keep order or prevent the rules from being broken, it is impossible to have a real game at all.

Just so, a nation of lawbreakers is no nation at all. It is a free-for-all fight, with the strongest getting away with everything worth having. It is only because America is a nation of law-observers, with only a very few lawbreakers, that our government is a success. Try to imagine what your street would be like if everyone along it was a burglar and a murderer. Life would not be worth living and no number of policeman could make life safe. This fact should serve to remind each American as to why our founding fathers sought to protect and preserve the right of individuals and churches to spread the teachings of Biblical morality and ethics throughout our nation.

Therefore, every American is in honor bound to obey the law. Arrest and punishment may or may not be around the corner if he breaks the law. The good American obeys the law because that is his God-given duty (Romans 13:1-7, 1 Peter 2:13-17). Obeying the law is part of the price that he gladly pays for living in a free and happy land.

All the precious liberties which we have studied demand self-control and respect for other people's rights on the part of each of us. Religious liberty, for instance, can amount to nothing unless every one respects his neighbor's right to worship God as he wills. Liberties mean equal duties, as we have seen. It is the old idea of fair play again. We can have our chance only because others let us have it; and, in turn, we must respect their chance when it comes. Liberty is something that you cannot have unless you are first willing to give it away.

There is a special and added reason for obeying the law in a free nation which every boy and girl should understand. It is our laws that we are obeying; laws that we made through our legislators whom we choose with our votes. So, too, it is our property that we destroy when we injure a park tree or destroy a public sign. A park is a piece of property that we all own together. Every child owns a share in it. Therefore every child with sense respects it and treats it with care, so that it will be preserved for his use and enjoyment. To needlessly destroy a park tree is just about as senseless as to throw your own baseball into the river.

6. **Pray** – It is the duty of all people to pray for their leaders and national prosperity. Almighty God requires all manner of men to worship and serve Him. However, Christians living in America have a particularly important duty to lead other citizens to pray for their leaders. God's people must lead by example and by precept in this regard. The Bible clearly states in 1 Timothy 2:1-3, "I exhort therefore, that, first of all, supplications, prayers, intercessions, and giving of thanks, be made for all men; for kings, and for all that are in authority; that we may lead a quiet and peaceable life in all godliness and honesty. For this is good and acceptable in the sight of God our Saviour."

Questions on the Text

1. What are the six chief duties of every American?
2. What does the duty of voting require besides casting a ballot, and how can that duty be met?
3. Why are taxes needed?
4. Should we always support every tax that civil government issues?
5. Why must every American serve as a juror when called?
6. What has fighting done for America?
7. Why should we obey the laws?
8. What sort of life would we lead if no one obeyed the laws?
9. By whom are American laws made?

Questions for Discussion

1. Why are boys and girls not allowed to vote?
2. How many of your relatives served in the Second World War?
3. How many laws do you know?
4. What public property is there in your city or village?
5. How many parks are there?
6. What rights of others can you think of that you must respect?
7. How can you pray specifically for someone you know who has been elected to serve in government?

CHAPTER 8

Home Rule

Two Uniforms – There are two government officers that every boy and girl sees daily on the street. They both wear uniforms. They both render important and familiar services to us all. They are the policeman and the postman.

At first sight, you might think there was no special difference between these two public servants, except the particular work they did. But there is one other difference that is most important and packed with meaning. If you understand this difference and the reason for it, you will understand a very large part of American government. You will gain an idea that goes to the roots of our whole system.

You can discover this important fact for yourself. Look at a postage stamp and you will find on it the words: "U. S. Postage." Look on the policeman's shield and you will find the name of your city: New York, Chicago, Los Angeles, Dallas, Atlanta, or your town, however small. The name of the locality is there - but no "U. S."

The Two Kinds of Work. – This is not mere chance. It has a far-reaching cause. Can you work it out for yourself? Why should the postman be an officer of the United States, of the national government at Washington; and the policeman an officer of your local government? Is not the reason fairly clear when you come to think of it? The policeman's job is wholly local. He has his beat, which may change, but his work never takes him out of the locality. It is local peace, local order, that he is to preserve. So he is hired and paid by the local government, the town, or city where you live. The postman, on the other hand, is part of a vast system that covers the whole country. Your particular postman's job is local enough, to deliver letters on a given street or route. But the letters he delivers come from all over the United States, and all over the world. He is one small cog in a great machine which has to be unified and under one central control to work well. Naturally, he is hired and paid by the national government, the United States Postal Service (formerly the Post-Office Department until 1970), in Washington, D.C.

The Principle of Local Government – Now, the great, general rule of America is to let each community do just as much governing as it safely can.   The principle of home rule as this is often called, is an idea which should be held deeply by every American. It goes back to our whole notion of personal liberty and the right of each individual to run his own concerns.

In the Family – Self-control or self-government is the beginning of home rule. Every American boy and girl is trusted far more than other children. It is the American way to put children on their honor as far as possible, to let them learn the value of money by using and saving it, to run their games, and generally take responsibility early. There are, of course, many things in which parents and teachers must give orders, and children must obey implicitly. However, whenever possible, Americans prefer to let their children learn by choosing and deciding for themselves. This system, we believe, produces self-reliant men and women, rich in individual character, common sense, and what is called "initiative." This word means the ability to act alone, on one's own ideas, without prodding from someone else. Americans are self-starters, we like to think.

Centralized Government – This principle applies not only in the home but all the way up, through each division of the country, in village, town, county, city, and State. You can see that the country might still be a democracy and be run on quite the reverse principle. All the power might be centralized at Washington. Your policeman might be hired by the government at Washington just as is the postman. That is, in fact, very much the way the French government is run.

The American Theory – But this is not the American way. Our theory is exactly that of home rule; that each community ought to run as much of its local affairs as possible. In this way, Americans learn about public affairs and become self-reliant citizens, able to vote more wisely on the great national questions that arise. You can see that this is the self-government theory over again. America tries to develop self-reliance in its communities exactly as it does in its boys and girls.

The Fifty United States – States are the essential framework of home rule in our government. They are something far more than mere areas of square miles, physical divisions into which the nation is carved. They are living parts of our national being, as complete in themselves and as necessary and vital to the life of the nation, as the nine individual players are necessary to a ball team. That is why they are all symbolized separately in the flag, each by a star, and the thirteen original States by a stripe as well.

Without the States, each leading a life of its own, it is doubtful if our nation could endure. It was the prediction of European observers that no nation as vast as ours could long exist as a republic. That it has done so and has prospered is due, first of all, to this basic American idea of a union of States; all endowed with full power of home rule. In our original system, the States were all independent governments loosely connected by a set of laws known as the *Articles of Confederation.*

Our God had everything to do with the creation of this unit at the start. As you know, there were thirteen colonies at the time of the Revolution; and these thirteen colonies became the thirteen original States. Our forefathers voluntarily united these separate governments into one government, which they called the "United States of America." The name recorded exactly what happened. "Federal" is another word often used to describe this fact in our government, that it was formed of several governments united into one government. The Latin motto *E pluribus unum,* which is on our coins, meaning "One from many," expresses the same idea.

There was no effort to destroy any part of the State governments. These on-going concerns were accepted of necessity. The problem that faced the wise, far-seeing, and patient men who met in the Constitutional Convention of 1787 was how to give full home rule to each of these separate States; and yet, so firmly unite them in a single nation that no quarrel from without or within could ever break them apart. How marvelously successful they were, time has proved. William Ewart Gladstone, the great Englishman, declared that the American Constitution was "the most wonderful work ever struck off at a given time by the brain and purpose of man." That is the general opinion of mankind.

The National Government – You see, then, the general scheme of our government. You can easily work out some of the details yourself. The mails were put in the charge of the federal government (that is the government in Washington, D.C.) for the obvious reason suggested before. Mails had to travel between States and, of course, no one State could handle them efficiently. All commerce between States (interstate commerce, as it is called, is Latin for "between-state") was placed under national control. The coining of money, which has to circulate in every State, was placed under federal control. The power to declare war and control of the army, navy, and air force was also given to the national government. Otherwise, as you can see, the separate States might have quarrelled as they pleased and there would have been no real nation at all. Also, the national government received the important power to raise money by taxation to pay for its Constitutionally mandated expenses. (You will remember from your American history that after the Revolution, from 1783 to 1788, when the Constitution was adopted, the country nearly fell to pieces under the Articles of Confederation which gave the central government no power to raise money and, otherwise, tied its hands).

Later on, the other powers of the national government will be stated in full. The point for you to see now is their general aim and character.

Power of the States – All the remaining powers of local government were left with the State governments, which thus received a free hand to run their local concerns very much as they wished. Therefore each State in the Union is a government by itself, with very great powers within its own area. (The police power is one of these powers, and that is how, as we discovered before, your policeman never happens to have "U. S." on his shield, but always the name of the locality.) This is home rule on a gigantic scale. California can build its roads and run its schools and pass laws about marriage and divorce and what-not to suit its situation and people, as can Louisiana, Minnesota, and Maine. Think how vast a country America is, how many different kinds of people there are in it, and how different the States are in climate, resources, and occupations; and you will see how useful and necessary it is that this sweeping home rule exists. It is safe to say that without this home rule by States, America never would have hung together and become the great nation that it is.

Home Rule within States – What did the States do with all these powers? Part of their freedom was to run their governments as they chose (within certain limits), therefore, no two State governments are exactly alike–the names of divisions vary, the names of officers vary, whole systems vary. We shall go into these divisions within the States in detail later. It is enough to say now that the same principle of home rule is respected and carried out in every State. The powers that a State possesses are passed on to its counties, its cities, its towns, and its villages.

To go back to your policeman, a State could, if it chose, hire all the policemen throughout its cities and villages; appointing them by its central government at its State capital. But no State does. Every State turns over this police power to the local government of city, county, village, or town. Nevertheless, most States retain a small police force that is under their direct control. These police often concentrate on governing highways and special investigations.

So we end where we began, with local government as the life-saving provision of American government, a living part of the structure of the original government through the preservation of the existing States, and an honored principle of government from one end of the country to the other.

Good and Bad Government – Under this system, each community gets just as good or just as bad a government as it deserves. If the voters of a village are intelligent and interested in their local government, if they watch it carefully and do their share of work, that village will be excellently governed. If the voters are illiterate and stupid and too lazy to vote or pay attention to public affairs, their village will be poorly governed.

What is true of a village is true of a city or a State. And it is not less true of the whole nation. A republic is not a short cut to good government. It is no cure-all. It simply enables a people fit for self-government to rule themselves as they deserve, without having to follow laws that were written by some bureaucrat who knows little about needs at the local level.

Questions on the Text

1. What important difference is there between the lettering on a postage-stamp and the lettering on a policeman's shield?
2. Why should the postman be an officer of the national government and the policeman an officer of the city or village?
3. What does the principle of home rule grant to each community?
4. How does it apply in the family?
5. What is a centralized government and what nation has this type of government?
6. Why do Americans believe in home rule?
7. What units of our government existed before the Revolution?
8. How many were there then and how many are there today?
9. How important are the States to the life of the nation?
10. What does "federal" mean?
11. What was the problem that faced the Constitutional Convention of 1787?
12. Name as many powers of the national government as you can.
13. Name as many powers of the States as you can.
14. Is the principle of home rule carried out within each state?
15. In America, what determines whether a community is governed well or badly?

Questions for Discussion

1. How many things does your city or village do?
2. Was your State one of the thirteen original States?
3. If so, how long before the Revolution was it settled?
4. If not, when did it enter the Union as a State?
5. Why is it important for each level of government (local, State, federal) to have enumerated/limited powers that are clearly defined?

Test 2

AMERICA'S CHRISTIAN HERITAGE

"...we ought to be no less persuaded that the propitious smiles of Heaven can never be expected on a nation that disregards the eternal rules of order and right which Heaven itself has ordained."

GEORGE WASHINGTON April 30, 1789

George Washington
(1732 - 1799)

Citizen farmer, surveyor, soldier, statesman, commander-in-chief of the Continental Army, first president of these United States of America. *"First in war, first in peace, first in the hearts of his countrymen."*

Hero of the 1755 Battle of Monogahela (French & Indian Wars), George Washington served in the historic Virginia House of Burgesses (1759 - 1774). An active and prayerful Christian, he was chosen vestryman of his local Anglican parish and became a practising Episcopalian after the War for Independence.

Washington was elected delegate to the First and Second Continental Congresses (1774, 1775). As Commander-in-Chief of the Continental Army, General Washington proved himself to be a stern disciplinarian, compassionate leader, and brilliant tactician. *"His diary, and his words and letters during the war years show him to have been a man of deep Christian faith.. . . "* [1]

Because the weaknesses of the Articles of Confederation resulted in anarchy and chaos in the new nation, Washington was prominent in the call for a federal government which could uphold law and justice at home and demand respect abroad. (Although he sought a stronger federal government to preserve the hard-won independence of the United States, he was a classical republican who sought to uphold the God-given rights of the people.) He insisted that all proper power be reserved to the sovereign states and the people thereof. He symbolized the importance of leaders being models of virtue and propriety.

In 1787, Washington was chosen to be president of the Constitutional Convention, a post which he accepted reluctantly. *"Believing that God had not only providentially spared his life on numerous occasions, but had also given him the victory over the British, the General* [accepted because he] *was convinced that God would hold him accountable for the future direction of American history."* [1]

George Washington was unanimously chosen to be the First President of the United States of America. Although he longed to return to private life at his beloved Mt. Vernon, he accepted his nation's call out of a deep sense of duty. "[Washington] *both embodied and knew the direct connection between Christianity and morality, and and the preservation of liberty."* [1]

---

[1] Quoted from "HOME EDUCATED AMERICAN STATESMEN, George Washington: The Father of His Country," by Archie P. Jones, *The Christian Educator,* Christian Liberty Academy © 1986 PRF.

The President

1. Term and Powers

Open to All – The presidency of the United States is the greatest office in the world, for which neither nobility nor riches are required. Any American boy or girl, however poor and whoever his or her parents may be, famous or unknown, can hope to become President. The only important restriction is that the President must have been born an American. (A naturalized citizen cannot be President.) It is also required that he be not less than thirty-five years old and have resided not less than fourteen years in the country. (Constitution, Art. II, Sec. 1, Par. 4)

The Executive Branch – As we saw before, the President corresponds to the captain of a team, leading the nation and seeing that the laws are carried out– which means "executing the law," in the language of the Constitution. From this the office of the President is usually described as the "executive branch" of our government; just as Congress, our lawmaking body, is called the "legislative branch;" and the courts, our umpires, are called the "judicial branch." The first and highest duty of the President is to "take care that the laws be faithfully executed" (Art. II, Sec. 3).

Term and Powers – The President is one of the most powerful rulers in the world. But two important facts must be kept in mind.

First, he is elected for a term of four years (Art. II, Sec. 1), and at the end of that time, unless the people wish him to continue in office, he loses all power and becomes a plain citizen like everyone else. Presidents can be re-elected for a second term but, since the ratification of the Twenty-second Amendment in 1951, they are no longer able to serve more than two terms. Prior to this amendment, all Presidents, except Franklin Roosevelt (who was elected President of the United States four times), followed George Washington's example by only serving two terms. George Washington refused a third term because it might have made him seem like a king.

Second, his powers are not anything he chooses, but, as you will see, only the definite things set down in black and white in the Constitution as his to do. These are the safeguards that prevent a President from becoming a tyrant or setting up anything like a monarchy.

Commander-in-Chief – "The President shall be commander-in-chief of the Army and Navy of the United States," says the Constitution (Art. II, Sec. 2). This means that he ranks above all our generals and admirals, and that every battleship, sailor, and soldier are his to command. During World War II, in the southwest Pacific , the Allied armies were originally placed under General MacArthur, thus achieving "unity of command," as it was called. Our fighting forces are run on this same principle, that one man, the President, must have complete control. He chooses the generals, the admirals; and directs the entire movements of our armies and fleets. You can see that this, alone, gives the President of the United States a vast power.

He Cannot Declare War – Yet right here you can understand how carefully the President's powers, great as they are, have been limited so as to safeguard the people's rights. The President makes war for us through our armies, navies, and air force but he cannot start a war. The power to declare war is reserved to Congress, composed of the House and Senate, our national legislature. Moreover, the President has no power to raise money to build ships or buy guns or anything else for the army or navy. Congress has the sole right to raise money by taxation and give it to the President for these purposes. So you see that while the President commands our army, navy, and air force, he cannot say whom they shall fight or when.

Division of Powers – This division of powers between President and Congress (and the courts, as you will see later) is one of the basic ideas of our government. The object is to prevent any one branch of the government from taking too much power and becoming tyrannical. You can observe this same purpose in much that follows. You will notice, for instance, that all important appointments made by the President must be approved by the Senate. This is a sweeping restriction on the entire executive power. Yet, since the power of removal is given wholly to the President, his control over his subordinates is complete.

2. The Cabinet

The Cabinet – The President could not possibly do all his duties himself, and Congress has authorized him to appoint fourteen secretaries in charge of as many departments. These are his official advisers and assistants, and are known as his Cabinet, though not so named in any law. The President presides over the Cabinet meetings which are held at frequent intervals. What goes on in these meetings is confidential, and no record of them is published. Each of these secretaries receives a salary.

The fourteen members of the Cabinet are:

1. Secretary of State, 1789
2. Secretary of the Treasury, 1789
3. Attorney General, 1789 (Department of Justice)
4. Secretary of the Interior, 1849
5. Secretary of Agriculture, 1889
6. Secretary of Commerce, 1913 (Commerce and Labor, 1903)
7. Secretary of Labor, 1913 (Commerce and Labor, 1903)
8. Secretary of Defense, 1947 (Departments of War and Navy, 1789)
9. Secretary of Housing and Urban Development, 1965
10. Secretary of Transportation, 1967
11. Secretary of Energy, 1977
12. Secretary of Health and Human Services, 1979 (Health, Education & Welfare)
13. Secretary of Education, 1979 (Health, Education and Welfare, 1953)
14. Secretary of Veterans Affairs, 1989

These are set down in the order of their creation by Congress, with the years of their beginning. This order is used for formal and ceremonial purposes, and it determines the line of Presidential succession for the Cabinet members. They also show how the business of the government has grown with the country. Congress defines the powers of each secretary; but the President appoints them and can remove them at will. The Senate must approve the appointment of each secretary.

Secretary of State – The President has general charge of the foreign affairs of the nation. That is to say, he negotiates treaties (agreements with other countries), sends out ambassadors and consuls to represent the United States in foreign countries, issues passports (travelling papers) to our citizens who wish to go abroad, and protects our citizens and ships wherever they may be. The Secretary of State runs these affairs for him.

But here again is a notable case of limiting the President's power; for all treaties must be approved by a two-thirds vote of the Senate before they are binding, and the appointment of all ambassadors, etc., must be approved by a majority vote of the Senate. The makers of our Constitution felt that a treaty, being an agreement with another nation which might bring us into grave difficulties, perhaps even war, should take effect only when thus carefully considered and accepted by another branch of government (Art. II, Sec. 2, Par. 2).

The Secretary of State is regarded as one of the highest and most important officers in the country. In many respects, he or she ranks next to the President in honor. Thomas Jefferson was Secretary of State under President Washington, and James Madison under President Jefferson.

Secretary of the Treasury – As the head of the Treasury Department, he handles all the money affairs of the national government. He collects the tariff (the tax on goods entering the United States from other countries) and all other federal taxes (such as income taxes through the Internal Revenue Service). He pays out money for all the expenses of the government. He raises money by loans (such as the Liberty Loans during World War I) or government bonds. He coins our money, through a subordinate known as the director of the mint, and has general direction of the national banks and the Federal Reserve banks.

In all these matters the President, and the secretary under him, can only carry out or execute the laws which Congress passes. That is to say, they can collect only the taxes that Congress orders and pay out only the money that congress directs. The President, for example, can build a post office only if Congress orders it and grants the money for it.

The Treasury Department also has charge of several other interesting departments: the Secret Service, to arrest counterfeiters and other violators of national laws, and now is most often associated with guarding the President; the Bureau of Engraving and Printing, to produce money, bonds, bills, notes, postage stamps, and food coupons; and formerly the Coast Guard from 1915 to 1967. The Bureau of Alcohol, Tobacco, and Firearms (BATF) is also under this department. This agency administers federal law as it affects these three areas.

Secretary of Defense – He is in charge of the Army, Navy, Marine Corps, and

Air Force. He is responsible for the nation's military affairs as he carries out the orders of the President, who is the nation's commander-in-chief. The Secretary of Defense is assisted by the Secretaries of the Army, Navy, and Air Force and the top military officers of the Army, Navy, Air Force, and Marine Corps, called the Joint Chiefs of Staff. The Department of Defense headquarters is at the Pentagon in Arlington, Virginia.

Each of the armed forces has its own college to train its regular officers. Each congressional district sends one student to each college, who is named by the representative of the district, usually after a competitive examination. Senators and the President also make a limited number of appointments. The United States Naval Academy is located at Annapolis, Maryland; the United States Air Force Academy is at Colorado Springs, Colorado; and the Army's college is the United States Military Academy at West Point, New York. Marine Corps officers are trained at the Naval Academy.

Attorney General – This officer has charge of the Department of Justice and gives legal advice to all the departments of the government and acts as their lawyer in court. He or she oversees the Bureau of Prisons and the Federal Bureau of Investigation (FBI). The Attorney General is also responsible for helping immigrants who enter the country and apply for naturalization, and to prevent illegal entry of aliens. The Antitrust Division, which prevents large corporations from forming monopolies, and the Drug Enforcement Agency fall under this jurisdiction.

Secretary of the Interior – This important secretary has charge of a number of miscellaneous internal affairs of the nation: the survey and gift or sale of the public lands; the national parks; the reclamation of arid lands by irrigation; helping American Indians, especially on reservations, to improve their health, education and welfare; geological survey of mineral deposits, height of mountains and the flow of water in rivers; looking for better and safer ways of mining natural resources, recycling solid wastes, and reclaiming damaged land; protecting wild animals and manages wildlife refuges; and guiding development of U.S. territories overseas.

The United States' most important territories are the Commonwealth of Puerto Rico, Guam, American Samoa, and the Virgin Islands. The residents of each of these territories elect their own governor and legislature to govern their own internal affairs. Each of these territories, along with the District of Columbia, elect one representative to the United States House of Representatives; although the representatives can only vote in committee. The United States also controls several small islands in the Pacific Ocean. A few have little or no permanent residents and are used solely for military purposes.

Secretary of Agriculture – His department maintains stations, at which it experiments with seeds and animals and spreads the knowledge thus gained among farmers. It also includes the Forest Service and two important bureaus that inspect foods and drugs to make sure that they are pure and wholesome. This department is responsible for supporting minimum prices for farm products, as well. Finally, the Food and Nutrition Service administers food stamps for those in need under this department's direction.

Secretary of Commerce – His department restocks lakes, rivers and the sea with fish. It also takes the census every ten years, now a colossal work, since the country has grown. One of the primary purposes of the census is to determine the number of representatives that each State should have in the House of Representatives. He also handles patents on useful devices which protect inventors for a period of 17 years, as well as trademarks which are protected for 20 years at a time. The National Weather Service is also under the control of this department.

Secretary of Labor – This department investigates the conditions of labor and promotes the welfare of workers. As we shall see, the regulation of labor conditions is primarily a State affair under the Constitution, and the powers of this national office are limited chiefly to advice. The Bureau of Labor Statistics is responsible for gathering statistical information regarding the effects of labor and employment practices. The Occupational Safety and Health Administration (OSHA) enforces codes that seek to protect the safety of workers. The Employment Standards Administration enforces federal law that relates to minimum wages, overtime pay, equal pay, and child labor.

Secretary of Health and Human Services – This office oversees the government's efforts to improve the economic security and physical health of every citizen of the United States. He is in charge of Social Security which provides retirement and survivors' income, as well as disability and health insurance for the elderly and needy. The Public Health Service, headed by the Surgeon General, conducts research, enforces quarantines, and examines immigrants. Centers for Disease Control, the Food and Drug Administration, Medicare, and Medicaid are all under the Department of Health and Human Services.

Secretary of Housing and Urban Development – The primary job of this secretary is to administer programs that help urban communities with their housing needs, through guaranteed mortgages and rent subsidies. He also allows for community development grants and encourages private investment, which creates new jobs and increased tax revenues.

Secretary of Transportation – The head of the Department of Transportation seeks to ensure safe, economical, and efficient transportation by land, water, or air. There are nine major divisions, which include aviation, highways, railroads, and seaways.

The United States Coast Guard is an important part of our seaway system. It protects lives and property at sea by maintaining navigational aids, watching out for icebergs, and providing assistance during shipping accidents. The Coast Guard is also responsible for enforcing all federal laws and treaties at sea and on the inland waterways. During times of war or national emergency, the Coast Guard supports the Navy. Since its establishment in 1790, the Coast Guard has been involved with the Navy in all of our wars. The Coast Guard also maintains the U.S. Coast Guard Academy at New London, Connecticut, for the training of its officers. Applicants must apply directly to the Coast Guard Academy—congressional appointments are not accepted.

The Federal Aviation Administration is another important agency. It enforces safety rules and supports a nationwide system of air-traffic control and navigation. Ultimately, all air travel in the United States falls under the jurisdiction of the FAA.

Secretary of Energy – He is responsible for directing federal policies and regulations regarding all aspects of the production, distribution, and consumption of energy in the United States. One of the DOE's most important jobs is to coordinate all federal activities relating to energy research and development.

Secretary of Education – The federal government's role in public education was increased through the Department of Education, by providing financial aid for elementary through secondary schools, and for handicapped, disadvantaged and gifted children. However, public education has continued to decline since the 1960's in spite of the federal government's attempts to financially support and legally favor public schools at the State level. This department recommends various policies or procedures for departments of education at the State level.

In addition, this department supports educational research, compiles statistics, and plans international teacher exchanges. It also runs a worldwide network of schools for children of military and diplomatic personnel.

Secretary of Veterans Affairs – The Department of Veterans Affairs (VA) has the second largest civilian work force (next to the U.S. Postal Service) which serves over 50 million veterans and their dependents. The nation's largest medical system is managed by the VA, and provides medical and dental services, hospital treatment, home nursing, physical therapy, and counseling. The VA also helps to train veterans for new jobs; handles pension payments and provides life insurance, and loans for homes and education for veterans.

3. Other Offices

Independent Agencies and Commissions - In addition to the fourteen departments, there are many other separate agencies and commissions which play an important role in our lives. A few of the more important are: the United States Postal Service which delivers our mail; the Interstate Commerce Commission which regulates railroads, trucks, and waterways; the Environmental Protection Agency which is responsible for developing and enforcing standards for controlling pollution; the Central Intelligence Agency which coordinates the foreign intelligence activities of the United States; and the Federal Reserve Board of Governors which sets the monetary policy of the United States.

Executive Office of the President - The Executive Office of the President was formed in 1939 by President Franklin Roosevelt to assist him in carrying out the growing demands on the President. The staff of the Executive Office often have greater influence on policy than secretaries of the various departments because they have greater access to the President, and because the President will often appoint his friends to these positions.

Two of the most important agencies within the Executive Office are the Office of

Management and Budget, and the National Security Council. The Office of Management and Budget prepares the annual budget for Congress and coordinates policies between the various departments and agencies. The National Security Council works with the Central Intelligence Agency, the Department of Defense, and the Department of State to coordinate the security functions of the United States; including intelligence gathering, crisis management, and policy formulation.

Library of Congress - This great library, founded in 1800 to serve the needs of Congress, is housed in a magnificent building near the Capitol in Washington. It is administered by the Librarian of Congress, who is appointed by the President. The Librarian issues copyrights for such things as books, plays, music, and computer software. Copyrights give writers the same exclusive right to profit from their work that patents give inventors.

4. Civil Service

Spoils System - "Civil Service" is a concept you should understand. "Civil" has many meanings. Here it means nothing more than "not-military." That is, the "civil service" of the government includes all office-holders not in the armed forces. Almost all of them were chosen by the President, and you can see what a task it would be if each new President appointed a new man for each job. That was the system for many years—the "spoils system," as it was called, based on the idea that "to the victor belong the spoils." As a party came into power, its President threw out all the office-holders not of his party, and rewarded his political friends with jobs.

Merit Selection - In 1883, however, a civil-service law called the Pendleton Act was passed which ended much of this. It has been extended year-by-year. This law provides that public offices must be filled on the basis of merit after examinations, just like school examinations; and when once chosen, an officer holds his job during good behavior. No one can be thrown out to make room for a politician. Today, the old Civil Service Commission has been replaced by the Office of Personnel Management; and administers the recruitment, examination, and training of some 3 million federal government workers.

The President still has a large number of appointments to fill, however, and this forms a large part of his duty. The most important appointments must be confirmed by the Senate, including the fourteen members of his Cabinet: the federal judges (including the justices of the Supreme Court); and U.S. district attorneys (who prosecute criminals); ambassadors, and consuls (Art. II, Sec. 2, Par. 2).

5. Legislative Powers

President and Congress – All this, so far, you will observe, is executive power. Congress passes a law under one of its constitutional powers, and the President carries it into action. We come now to an important part that the President plays in the making of laws.

The Veto – The word "veto" is Latin for "I forbid." Under our Constitution, when Congress has passed a bill, it must go before the President before it takes effect.

He can sign it, in which case it becomes a law at once. If he does nothing, it becomes a law after ten days, provided Congress is still sitting. If Congress adjourns within ten days, the President need do nothing. The bill fails unless he signs it. This is called the "pocket veto." He, also, can veto the bill, sending it back to Congress with any reasons he cares to give. This kills the bill.

Congress can take it up again if it wishes, but cannot pass it over the President's veto; except by a two-thirds vote of both Houses. As this vote is difficult to get, the President's veto is a very powerful obstacle to Congress. It compels Congress to pay attention to the President's views if it wishes its bills to become laws, and gives the President a very decided influence on all legislation. A strong and courageous President has more influence than a weak one, but the power is very real and important in any President's hands.

Here, you will notice, the Constitution places a very important check upon Congress and its whole legislative power (Art. I, Sec. 7, Pars. 2 and 3).

Messages to Congress – The Constitution provides that the President shall "from time-to-time give to the congress information of the state of the Union, and recommend to their consideration such measures as he shall judge necessary and expedient." (Art. II, Sec. 3.) George Washington delivered his messages to Congress orally. Jefferson, not caring for public speaking, sent his messages in writing; and that continued to be the custom down to President Wilson who resumed the forgotten practice of addressing Congress in person. The President usually sends an annual message and as many shorter messages as he deems proper. This right is not nearly as effective as the power of the British Prime Minister, who sits in the British House of Commons and leads its debates, but it adds considerably to the President's influence upon legislation.

Special Sessions of Congress – The President can call Congress in special session to consider any subject that he considers important whenever he wishes. This gives him an added influence upon Congress, for he can keep Congress sitting as long as he wishes. (Art. II, Sec. 3.)

These three powers: to veto bills, to send messages to Congress, and to call special sessions of Congress are the only legislative powers of the President.

6. Judicial Power

Pardoning Power – The President has another power, which is judicial. He can pardon any criminal convicted under a federal law - that is, for example: mail thieves, counterfeiters, or smugglers. There are no constitutional limits on this power, but no President uses it except to free a man who has been wrongly or too harshly punished; to correct the errors of courts, in other words (Art. II, Sec. 2, Par. 1).

7. Election

Election of President – This is one of the few provisions of the Constitution which has not worked out as the makers of the Constitution hoped. They planned an

AMERICA'S CHRISTIAN HERITAGE

"...the religion which has introduced civil liberty, is the religion of Christ and His apostles. This is genuine Christianity and to this we owe our free constitutions of government." **NOAH WEBSTER 1833**

Noah Webster
(1758 - 1843)

Noah Webster was one of the most influential men during the early years of the American Republic. His work helped to establish an American system of education which would support America's Christian philosophy of government.

Webster was raised in a home in which the foundations of Christian self-government, individual responsibility, and Biblical work habits were firmly implanted. When his parents mortgaged the family farm to send him to Yale, their benediction to young Noah read, in part: "We wish to have you . . . so live as to obtain the favor of Almighty God and His grace in this world . . ." So it was that this young man who bore a Biblical name became "an <u>ark</u> in which the American Christian spirit rode the deluge of rising anti-Christian and anti-republican waters which threatened to inundate the nation" in the late 1700's and early 1800's.

A prolific writer, he never wavered from the theme of American Christian morality and patriotism. During the 100 years in which generations used his *American Spelling Book* (the "blue-backed speller"), more than <u>100 million copies</u> were printed. He also edited the first American revised version of the Bible. His *History of the United States* (1832) traced the relationship of America to Christianity and The Bible, and God's hand in the forging of the republic.

Noah Webster's greatest work was *The American Dictionary of the English Language,* first published in 1828. It established a Biblical system of language in which the meaning of words were largely drawn from The Scriptures -- as indeed was then common American practice. His work served to establish our distinctive national language.

The blessing of that dictionary today is that it serves as a repository of the three essential properties of our American heritage: a Christian philosophy of life, government, and education. It also stands as the <u>primary</u> source for the original meaning of the Constitutional terms used by the framers of that vital document.

"In my view," wrote Noah Webster, "the Christian religion is the most important, and one of the first, things in which all children . . . ought to be instructed."

Noah Webster's legacy is this: He demonstrated the power and influence one individual can have if he or she is consciously dedicated to Christ and country.

Based on Rosalie J. Slater's preface to the facsimile edition of Noah Webster's First Edition of An American Dictionary of the English Language, Foundation for American Christian Education, 1967. Copyright 1986, PLYMOUTH ROCK FOUNDATION, Marlborough, NH 03455.

Electoral College of wise men chosen by the people, and gave the election of a President and Vice-President to this body. They did not trust the people to pick a good President directly. This body still exists, and when you vote for President you nominally vote only for "presidential electors." But these electors are selected by the parties who have already named their candidates for President and Vice-President, and they always vote as their parties wish. So your vote really counts for the candidate, and the Electoral College might just as well not exist. The Constitution still provides for the Electoral College, but the people vote directly for their President none-the-less. The original provision (Art. II, Sec. 1, Par. 2) was changed in 1804 by the Twelfth amendment, but not so as to eliminate the Electoral College. The vote for President was merely separated from the vote for Vice-President.

Minority Presidents – The only effect of preserving this peculiar provision is to sometimes make possible the election of a "minority President" - that is, a President who did not receive a majority of all the votes in the country. This is because the electors are chosen by the States and the District of Columbia. Each State has as many votes in the Electoral College as it has representatives and senators in Congress. The District of Columbia can never have more electors than the least populous State (Twenty-third Amendment). Now if one candidate carries a few States by very large majorities, and his opponent carries many States by very small majorities, the latter may easily win a majority in the Electoral College, and yet not have half of all the votes cast. Lincoln was a minority President in 1860. So have an additional eight other Presidents. This may seem unusual, but it is our historic method; and it has never been considered worthwhile to change.

Election by the House – The electors of each State meet at their own State capitol on the second Monday in January, following the election and vote. Their ballot is sent to the President of the Senate, and on the second Wednesday in February the President of the Senate, before a joint session of Congress, opens the ballots and they are counted.

A majority of the electoral vote is required; and therefore, if there is a tie or the votes are split among a number of candidates, the election fails. In this event, the election is thrown into the House of Representatives, which chooses a President from among the three candidates standing highest in the vote of the Electoral College. In this balloting, each State has one vote. The Senate elects a Vice-President under similar conditions. Twice the election has been thus thrown into the House, in 1800, when Jefferson and Burr were tied; and in 1824, when the electoral votes were divided among four candidates and John Quincy Adams was elected by the House.

Inauguration Day – The President is elected early in November (the Tuesday following the first Monday), every four years. But he does not take office until noon on January 20th of the following year, being known as Inauguration Day. The original date set by Congress for Presidential inaugurations was March 4th; but the Twentieth Amendment, adopted in 1933, changed the date to January 20th (Art. XX, Sec. 1). He then takes the oath of office set forth in the Constitution (Art. II, Sec. 1, Par. 7): "I do solemnly swear (or affirm) that I will faithfully execute the office of President of the United States, and will to the best of my ability preserve, protect, and defend the

Constitution of the United States." The oath is administered by the Chief Justice of the United States. This ceremony is preceded by a great parade and followed by a speech from the new President outlining his policies; delivered from the Capitol steps before a vast crowd. He is then driven to his new home, the White House. The President receives a salary which may not be changed during his time in office.

The President's Death – If the President dies or becomes disabled the Vice-President, elected at the same time with him, becomes President (Art. II, Sec. 1, Par. 5). Until that time, the Vice-President's main task is to preside over the Senate. If the Vice-President dies before the President, "the President shall nominate a Vice President who shall take office upon confirmation by a majority vote of both Houses of Congress" (Art. XXV, Sec. 2). However, if both the President and the Vice-President die at the same time, the Speaker of the House is next in line for the Presidency. The Congress has always had the right to change the order of succession if both the President and Vice-President die; but since 1947 the following order has been set: the Speaker of the House, the president *pro tempore* (now shortened to *pro tem*) of the Senate, followed by the Cabinet members in the order when each of their departments were created, starting with the Secretary of State.

Questions on the Text

Section 1

1. What are the Constitutional qualifications for the Presidency?
2. What are the three branches of the American government?
3. How long is the President's term?
4. Can he be re-elected?
5. Can the President rule the country as he wishes?
6. How does the Constitution provide for a unified command of the Armed Forces?
7. Who alone has the right to declare war?
8. Can the President raise money by taxation?
9. Why does the Constitution carefully divide powers between President and Congress, and what illustrations of this division can you give?

Section 2

10. How many members are there in the cabinet?
11. Describe a cabinet meeting.
12. How many departments can you name?
13. How many departments were created in 1789?
14. What are the matters of which the Secretary of State has charge?
15. What is a passport?
16. What are treaties and who negotiates them?
17. By whom must a treaty be ratified and by what vote before it is binding on the United States?
18. What has the Secretary of the Treasury charge of?
19. In what two ways can he raise government funds?

20.   What are the tasks of the Secret Service?
21.   What has the Secretary of Defense charge of?
22.   How are the cadets selected for the U.S. Military Academy at West Point?
23.   What does the Attorney General do?
24.   What internal affairs of the Secretary of the Interior can you name?
25.   What does the Department of Agriculture have charge of?
26.   What responsibilities of the Secretary of Commerce can you name?
27.   When is the census taken?
28.   What has the Secretary of Labor charge of?
29.   What is the Secretary of Health and Human Services responsible for?
30.   What has the librarian charge of at the Library of Congress?
31.   Which territories and possessions have legislatures of their own?

Section 3

32.   What is the purpose of the Interstate Commerce Commission?
33.   What function does the Central Intelligence Agency perform?

Section 4

34.   What does civil service mean? What is it called today?
35.   What is the spoils system and how does the civil service law end it?
36.   What appointments must be confirmed by the Senate?

Section 5

37.   What is the chief legislative power of the President?
38.   If exercised, what can Congress do?
39.   How are the Presidents messages to Congress delivered?
40.   Who can call Congress in special session?

Section 6

41.   Are there any limits to the President's pardoning power?
42.   What criminals does it touch?

Section 7

43.   What is the Electoral College?
44.   How has it worked out differently from the original plan?
45.   What is a minority President?
46.   Can you explain how such a President can be elected?
47.   What happens if no candidate has a majority in the Electoral College?
48.   When is the President elected and when does he take office?
49.   What happens on Inauguration Day?
50.   If the President and Vice-President should both die, who would succeed to the office?

Questions for Discussion

1. How many Presidents have been re-elected?
2. Has there ever been a President from your State?
3. Can you name any cabinet officers from your State?
4. How many present members of the cabinet can you name?
5. Why is it necessary for the Senate to ratify treaties made with foreign countries or international organizations?
6. What national parks can you name?
7. Have you ever seen a presidential message to Congress?
8. How many Presidents have died in office?
9. Has the succession ever gone beyond the Vice-President?

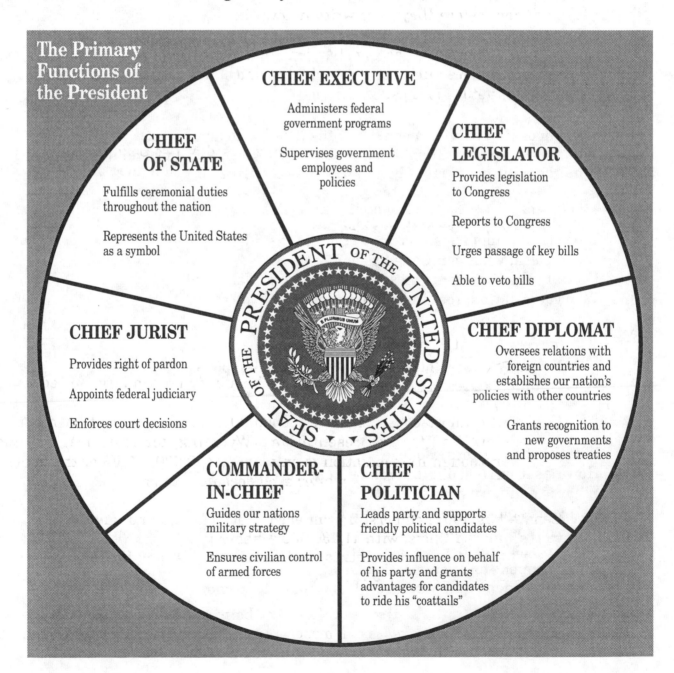

The Primary Functions of the President

CHIEF EXECUTIVE

Administers federal government programs

Supervises government employees and policies

CHIEF OF STATE

Fulfills ceremonial duties throughout the nation

Represents the United States as a symbol

CHIEF LEGISLATOR

Provides legislation to Congress

Reports to Congress

Urges passage of key bills

Able to veto bills

CHIEF JURIST

Provides right of pardon

Appoints federal judiciary

Enforces court decisions

CHIEF DIPLOMAT

Oversees relations with foreign countries and establishes our nation's policies with other countries

Grants recognition to new governments and proposes treaties

COMMANDER-IN-CHIEF

Guides our nations military strategy

Ensures civilian control of armed forces

CHIEF POLITICIAN

Leads party and supports friendly political candidates

Provides influence on behalf of his party and grants advantages for candidates to ride his "coattails"

Test 3

42

CHAPTER 10

Congress

1. The Two Houses

The Legislative Branch – The rules of baseball, as we saw, are made by a national commission representing the big leagues. Most of the rules are very old, and were followed by boys playing the game long before they were written down. But changes are made almost every year to meet new conditions or clear up doubts, and that is why a rule-making body is always needed. The laws of the United States are much the same. Many of them are very old and were customs, habits of right and fair-dealing among men, before they were written down into laws. But the country grows so rapidly, and the conditions of life are changing so constantly, that new laws are needed every year. Therefore, the Constitution created our Congress to sit every year in Washington, to debate our national problems and make our laws (subject to the President's right of veto). It is called the legislative branch of our government (Art. I, Sec. 1).

Two Houses of Congress – Congress is composed of two bodies, the House of Representatives (usually called the "House") and the Senate. One meets in one end of the Capitol Building; the other meets in the other side. A bill must be passed by both House and Senate before it can become a law. The two bodies are unlike in many important ways except that both are elected by the people.

The House of Representatives now contains 435 members, allotted to the States according to population. The Reapportionment Act of 1929 fixed the membership of the House at its present size. Thus the large States have many representatives; the small ones few. New York has 31 representatives, Delaware 1. Originally each State was allowed 1 representative for every 33,000 inhabitants, and this gave the first House 65 members. If this ratio had remained unchanged, the House would now consist of around 8,000 members, which would make a body far too large for effective deliberation. Congress has, therefore, increased the ratio from time to time. A representative is now allotted approximately 600,000 inhabitants. But each State, however small, is entitled to 1 representative (Wyoming, for instance, has one representative, even though its population is only about 450,000 – 75% of the quota). Congress fixes the ratio of representation after each decennial census (Art. I, Sec. 2).

The Senate has 100 members, 2 from each State. Large and small States are thus represented alike. Illinois, with 11,430,000 inhabitants, has two senators, and so has Alaska, with 550,000. It has increased in size only as new States have been admitted to the Union (Art. I, Sec. 3).

There are several other important differences between the House and Senate. A senator must be at least thirty years old; a representative need be only twenty-five. A senator is elected for a term of six years, a representative for only two years. Besides, all the representatives are elected at the same time and thus, go out of office at the same time; whereas in the Senate the terms are so arranged that only one-third are elected at any one election, two-thirds always holding over.

Why Two Houses – Can you see any reasons for having two legislative bodies that are so unlike each other? The explanation for one great difference is historical. As we saw before, when the federal government was formed in 1789, the original States came in with all their existing governments. They varied much in size, and local pride was very strong. The smaller States would not have come into the Union if the Senate had not been planned so as to give them equal power and prestige, and thus prevent the larger States from taking full control. The theory was that the Senate represented the States as governments. That is the first reason why large and small States have the same vote and power in the Senate.

But there are other and better reasons for having two houses and having the membership of one older in years and less frequently changed. The preparing and passing of good laws is a slow and difficult business requiring much thought and care. People are constantly having new ideas that sound well but that do not work out. If we had one legislative body, and that the House; new, untried, and ill-considered laws might be passed. With the Senate, we are sure of thorough debate, investigation, and careful decisions. They represent different points of view. Each is a check on the other. By the time both have agreed on a law, we can be fairly confident that it is a wise and just one.

The Capitol is where Congress meets to make the rules for the whole nation.

(Library of Congress)

The Capitol, Washington, D.C.

Direct Election of Senators – The Constitution originally had one additional device for making the Senate less likely to act hastily. It provided that, whereas representatives should be elected directly by the people, the senators should be chosen by the State legislatures. The thought was that, thus, more conservative and thoughtful men would be chosen. Also, this system accorded with the theory of the Senate as the representative of the States as governments. This did not meet the approval of Americans, and in 1913, by the Seventeenth Amendment to the Constitution, this was changed; and today our senators are elected as are the representatives, by popular vote.

Election of Representatives – Congress has provided that representatives must be elected by districts and not by the whole State ("at large," as this latter method is termed). Of course, in small States entitled to only one representative (as of 1992 these include Alaska, Delaware, Montana, South Dakota, North Dakota, Vermont, and Wyoming), he is elected by the voters of the whole State.

The States lay out these congressional districts as they wish, and much unfairness has been worked at times in the effort by a party in power to apportion the State to its advantage. The trick has been either to throw the greatest possible number of voters into one district, certain to vote a particular way, or to add a friendly area to an evenly divided district. Congressional districts have taken on extraordinary shapes as a result. The I - 85 district in North Carolina is a prime example, with a series of separate population centers connected only by Interstate 85. The device is called "gerrymandering," after Elbridge Gerry, Governor of Massachusetts (1812). He had helped redistribute the districts of his State so as to produce one district resembling an odd animal figure. "A salamander" was suggested. When Gerry was finished with his reapportionment, the salamander-shaped district was quickly dubbed a "gerrymander."

A representative is not required by law to live in the district that elects him. But custom demands it. It has been argued that abler men might be sent, if this restriction were not imposed, even though the local interests of the district might not be so closely regarded. The English custom, by contrast, frequently elects great national figures from districts where they do not live.

2. Powers

The Powers of Congress – Congress, like the President, is not free to do anything it wishes. It can do only what the Constitution expressly permits it to do. Its powers are mainly set forth in Section 8 of Article I of the Constitution. They are, the powers which the nation needs to preserve itself, and which the nation can exercise better than the States. All the other matters, affecting local concerns, are left to the States to handle as they think best. The chief provisions thus given to Congress to legislate about are as follows:

1. To collect taxes.
2. To borrow money.

3.   To regulate commerce with foreign countries and between the States.
4.   To coin money and punish counterfeiters.
5.   To establish post offices and post roads.
6.   To provide for patents and copyrights.
7.   To punish piracy and other crimes committed on the high seas.
8.   To declare war.
9.   To maintain an army and navy.
10.   To govern the Territories (Art. IV, Sec. 3) and the District of Columbia.
11.   To admit new States (Art. IV, Sec. 3).
12.   To make all the laws needed to carry into effect these powers.

As you see, under the last provision, Congress has been given a liberal grant of power with respect to the things it is permitted to do. Congress has a free hand in the jobs assigned to it. This has often been called "the elastic clause," because it has been stretched in some cases to cover a good deal. Those who believe that the national government should not increase in power, construe it very strictly. Those who would strengthen the national government construe it liberally. This is an old and perennial dispute between American political parties. The men who framed our Constitution believed that the power of government must be strictly limited because "the government that governs least governs best." However, many politicians today have forgotten this truth and have sought to expand the role of the federal government.

By referring to the tenth provision above, you can work out a good illustration of what Congress can and cannot do. For example, the District of Columbia has been granted home rule since 1974, but home rule can be revoked by Congress any time it wants to do so. (It was originally granted self-government in 1871 but had it revoked in 1874.) Congress retains final authority over the District and can override the District's budget and laws. In 1988, Congress forced the District of Columbia to repeal a law which had required Georgetown University to sanction homosexual organizations. The District's prosecutor and judges are still federal appointees.

It can do none of these local things in New York, Illinois, California or in any of the other States. In them it can only run the mails, draft soldiers, and do the other national things enumerated. All the other matters are left up to the States to do as their own State constitutions dictate.

As you have noticed, these provisions or powers granted to Congress cover, in very general terms, the things that the President through his Cabinet carries into action. The people adopted the Constitution; by it they gave Congress the power to make laws about certain things; and the President sees that such laws as are passed are carried out.

Congress and the Bill of Rights – As was stated in Chapter VI, Congress, with all its power, cannot pass any law interfering with the liberties of American citizens. Personal safety and freedom, religious freedom, free speech, property, and trial by jury, are all protected by what is often called the "Bill of Rights" in the

Constitution - the first Ten Amendments passed shortly after the original Constitution was adopted. Just how Congress is restrained will be explained in the next chapter on the courts.

Section 9 of Article I also ties the hands of Congress in certain similar respects, as, for instance, in prohibiting any title of nobility. Congress can not create a prince, duke, or earl, if it wanted to.

Special Powers of the House and Senate – As we saw before, the Senate has certain powers all its own. It can approve or reject treaties which the President makes with foreign countries (a two-thirds vote being necessary for approval). It can confirm or reject the President's appointments to certain high offices (the fourteen-member Cabinet, judges, ambassadors, etc.) as noted in the preceding chapter. From this power has grown a custom known as "senatorial courtesy;" whereby a President is expected to consult the senator of his own party in a State, if there is one, before making an appointment therein. Thus the senators have gained a large control over federal "patronage," as this selection of office-holders is called.

The only peculiar power of the House is that all the tax bills must start in it - this, because taxes hit all the people and the House is better able to speak for all the people at any given time than the senate. Once introduced in the House, tax bills must go to the Senate and be passed by the Senate like any other bills (Art. I, Sec. 7, Par. 1).

When a President or any federal officer violates the law or the Constitution, Congress can remove him by a trial known as "impeachment." In this the House accuses him and states the charges; and the Senate tries him, sitting as a court. But only one President has ever been thus tried, Andrew Johnson, and he was not convicted (Art. I, Sec. 2, Par. 5, and Sec. 3, Pars. 6 and 7). Johnson's case provides a good example of how unclear the impeachment clause is and how it may be used unfairly by certain politicians. Andrew Johnson wanted to quickly start the reconstruction process for the South, following the Civil War. His program was in keeping with Abraham Lincoln's desire "to bind up the nation's wounds." Because he did not want to deal harshly with the former Confederate States, the Radical Republicans opposed him with a Reconstruction program that punished the South. So the House drafted an impeachment bill, that was sent to the Senate, where Johnson was acquitted by one vote.

3. Organization

How Congress Works – The House elects a speaker who presides over its sessions. His position is one of great importance and influence. Any representative can propose any bill, meaning the draft of a law, that he wishes to. It is referred to a committee which can either kill it or, upon approval, report it back to the House for action. The House is divided into a large number of these committees, each with certain subjects assigned to it; and very important and decisive action takes place in these committees. One of the most important is the Ways and Means Committee, which approves all tax bills for the raising of revenue. The most powerful is the

Committee of Rules, which largely determines what bills shall be considered. The bill, if reported back by the committee, must be read three times on three different days. This ensures that no bill is slipped through unawares before it is voted upon. If it receives a majority of votes, it is sent to the Senate; which takes it up in just the same way—referring it to a committee, and so on. If the Senate passes the bill, it goes to the President for him to approve or veto. If the Senate does not pass it, the bill fails. Often the Senate amends, that is to say, changes the bill as it comes from the House. The matter then goes to a conference committee of representatives and senators, who try to adjust the differences and agree upon a compromise bill which can pass both House and Senate.

The Vice-President presides over the Senate, but he has no vote except when there is a tie. Bills are introduced in the Senate, referred to committees, and so on, exactly as in the House. The only restriction is that tax bills cannot be drafted in the Senate. Owing to its smaller size, the Senate is a much more effective forum for debate than the House. When the Seante is considering highly sensitive matters it goes into "executive session" and its proceedings are secret.

Congress used to meet every year on the first Monday in December (Art. I, Sec. 4, Par. 2). But now it first meets on January 3rd, according to the Twentieth Amendment, unless an alternate date is chosen by law (Art. XX, Sec. 2). It also meets in special session at other times, when the President summons it.

Questions on the Text

Section 1

1. Why is a legislature necessary?
2. How many representatives were there in the first House and how many today?
3. How many Americans did a member of the first House represent and about how many Americans does each member of the House represent now?
4. How many senators are chosen from each State?
5. What is the length of the terms in the House and the Senate, and what other differences are there in the composition of the two bodies?
6. What is the historical reason for our Senate?
7. What other reason is there for two legislative bodies?
8. How were senators originally elected and how are they now chosen?
9. How are representatives chosen and what is a gerrymander?

Section 2

10. What sort of powers has Congress?
11. How many powers can you name?
12. What is the "elastic clause"?
13. What control does Congress have over the District of Columbia?
14. What is the Bill of Rights and where is it found?

15. Can Congress create a noble?
16. What peculiar powers has the Senate?
17. Where must tax bills originate?
18. What is impeachment and how is it carried out?

Section 3

19. What do the committees of the House and Senate do?
20. Trace the passage of a bill from the time it is introduced till it becomes a law.
21. Who presides over the House and who over the Senate?
22. What is an executive session of the Senate?
23. When does Congress meet?

Questions for Discussion

1. Do you know the name of the representative from your congressional district and the names of the two senators from your State?
2. What is the population of your State and how many representatives has it?
3. What are the boundaries of your congressional district?
4. Why was President Johnson impeached?
5. Is Congress in session and when did it begin to sit?
6. Who is the speaker of the House?

Congressional Powers

THE SENATE   THE HOUSE OF
                                                    REPRESENTATIVES

DELEGATED POWERS

Collect taxes to pay for the cost of the federal government

Regulate trade with foreign nations

Regulate trade and industry among the states

Declare war and make peace

Raise armed forces to defend our nation

Establish post offices and roads

Print and coin money

Make rules about naturalization and immigration

Govern the District of Columbia

Admit new states to the Union

Borrow money

Establish a system of courts

Govern the impeachment of federal officers

IMPLIED POWERS

To make all laws "necessary and proper" to carry out the delegated powers

To "provide for the general welfare" of the United States

49

CHAPTER 11

The Federal Courts

The Need of National Judges – The simplest rules of baseball need an umpire to apply them, and you can see how great is the need of a fair and unbiased umpire to tell the President, Congress, and the people just what the Constitution means on any given subject. Disputes would be endless, otherwise. Even more important, Congress might claim power not really given it; it might pass a law taking away religious liberty or free speech or a man's life or property; and if there were no umpire to say no, the law would prevail.

Their Powers – The federal courts, of which the Supreme Court at Washington is the highest and final authority, act as this umpire. Their chief work is to interpret the Constitution, decide what it means, and if Congress has exceeded its powers to say so. When these courts decide that a law is not authorized by the Constitution, it is declared unconstitutional, and that law is wiped out. Similarly, if anybody violates the Constitution, a private citizen, a policeman, or even a State judge or a legislator, the federal courts step in and direct that the Constitution be obeyed. These courts are the bulwark of the Constitution. Without them, the Constitution could not protect our liberties or make our country a safe and happy place to live in.

These courts also settle disputes and punish crimes arising under the laws passed by Congress and under treaties with foreign nations. There are State courts which pass on the State laws enacted by State legislatures, as we shall see. Most crimes are local in character and are tried in the State courts. Thus, if a boy smashed a streetlight he would be breaking a local, that is, a State law, and would be tried in a State court. But if he stole a letter from a mail-box he would be breaking a federal law protecting the mails, which is a national concern, and would be tried in a federal court. Counterfeiters must similarly be tried in federal courts, for it is the federal law which punishes counterfeiting.

The federal courts hear certain other cases as well. All disputes between States come before them, also all suits between citizens of different States. The idea here is, that the federal court is better fitted to be impartial, since it is chosen by the President and not by either State. (Art. III, Sec. 1 and 2.)

The Supreme Court – This is the highest court in the land, and in many respects the most powerful court in the world. It has attempted to apply the Constitution to our changing and growing nation for more than two hundred years. Whenever the Supreme Court justices have sought to ignore the original intent of the Constitution, which has happened frequently in the last fifty years, they have engaged in the unconstitutional process of issuing legal opinions in the form of legislative edicts. In other words, this court has frequently attempted to create new laws by way of their opinions, instead of limiting their duties to striking down laws that are unconstitutional. This problem must be corrected before the Supreme Court loses its credibility. Membership on the Supreme Court is one of the highest honors in the country. The Chief Justice ranks as one of our most important public figures.

The court consists of the Chief Justice and eight associate justices. The Congress is responsible for determining the number of Supreme Court justices, since the Constitution does not specify. Originally, the Court had six justices in 1789; and after several changes, Congress settled on the present nine in 1869. They are appointed by the President (with the consent of the Senate) and serve for life. The court sits in the Capitol at Washington. Most cases come before it on appeal from the lower courts. That is to say, the side that loses at the first trial "appeals" to this higher court to have the decision changed. However, the Supreme Court may hear two types of cases on the first appeal: those involving ambassadors and other diplomats, and those in which a State is involved. The cases the Supreme Court hears on second appeal come from the highest State courts, the U.S. District Courts, and the Courts of Appeals.

District Courts and Courts of Appeals – The lowest federal courts, in which suits begin, are usually called district courts. These are the "workhorses" of the federal judiciary, handling over 100,000 cases each year (90% of all federal cases). Appeal is first made to the district courts over many different cases, including civil and criminal. Some civil cases involve bankruptcy, civil rights, and tax laws. On the other hand, some criminal cases which these courts might hear are bank robbery, counterfeiting, income tax evasion, and kidnapping.

The second level of the federal courts system consists of the Courts of Appeals, which was created in 1891 to handle the backlog of cases in the Supreme Court. There are eleven of these courts, each one covering at least three States. There are over one hundred and thirty judges that sit on the eleven courts. Most cases come from district courts, but they also may come from special courts (e.g., U.S. Tax Court) and regulatory agencies (e.g., Interstate Commerce Commission). The Courts of Appeals handles about 20,000 cases each year, which are usually the courts of last resort for most federal cases.

Questions on the Text

1. How do the federal courts see that the Constitution is obeyed?
2. What cases come before the federal courts?
3. What cases come before the State courts?
4. How many justices sit on the Supreme Court?
5. What are the other federal courts?

Questions for Discussion

1. Who was the greatest of our Chief Justices?
2. Who is the Chief Justice now? Can you name any of the associate justices?
3. Can you think of any other cases than those in the text that would naturally come before the federal courts?

51

CHAPTER 12

The Three Branches of Our Government

Our System of Checks and Balances – You have now seen the three branches of our government – the executive, the legislative, and the judicial – and you have seen in detail how they check each other. The legislative power of Congress is checked by the President's veto. The executive power of the President is checked by the Senate's right to reject his appointments. The judiciary can check Congress all along the line by its right to hold Congress responsible with respect to the Constitution. All this was carefully planned by the makers of our Constitution, with definite purposes in view. They called it a system of checks and balances.

Its Purposes – The purposes were two. One was to prevent tyranny by any one branch. The other was to prevent hasty action by the nation. If too much power lay in any one branch, or if the branches were not separate (e.g., the executive and legislative powers were united in one body, as is true in England today, where the chief executive is the Prime Minister chosen by the House of Commons), there would be the danger that some very strong man or men would usurp power and set up a dictatorship.

LEGISLATIVE

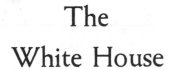

The White House

EXECUTIVE

JUDICIAL

The second reason does not appeal to some Americans with plans of change and reform. Undoubtedly, the system sometimes holds back desirable changes too long. It certainly compels delay, debate, and second thoughts. It has certainly prevented many blunders. If it errs on the side of "safety first," it has worked and worked successfully for many years, through all kinds of strain and stress. Even if it makes us impatient at times, we should realize its value, and hesitate a long time before changing it.

Questions on the Text

1. What illustrations of our system of checks and balances can you give?
2. What are the two objects of the system?
3. Why should we be slow to change it?

Test 4

CHAPTER 13

What the Nation Does For Us

1. Fundamental Services

In our Daily Life – Having viewed the machinery of our national government, let us examine in detail what services it renders each of us. Most of the things that come nearest to our daily life are done by the local government, as we shall find later. However, the national government does perform some very important services of this character such as the delivery of mail. As we know from our study of liberty and fair play, it also performs other services that are more important, even though they are not so easily seen and appreciated. Let us take up these less visible services first, since they have already been suggested.

The Greatest Service of All – Our strong national government protects all our rights of liberty: our safety and happiness, our religious freedom, and our free speech. Under a weak and unstable government, no man's life or property is secure from day to day. You have read in our own history how troubled the years were just after the Revolution, when the thirteen colonies were loosely held together under the Articles of Confederation. It was, in fact, the disorder and confusion of these years that made the colonies see the need and wisdom for a strong union under the Constitution. From 1783 to 1789, the new American confederation was threatened from without and from within; and the new Constitution gave the nation vast powers to end these troubles and safeguard the people's liberties. The Preamble to the Constitution states this clearly:

> *We the people of the United States, in order to form a more perfect union, establish justice, insure domestic tranquility, provide for the common defense, promote the general welfare, and secure the blessings of liberty to ourselves and our posterity, do ordain and establish this Constitution for the United States of America.*

Enemies Abroad – In times of peace, we are apt to forget that the most fundamental service of our national government is to provide for our nation's defense. Anyone who lived through the period of the Second World War can never make this mistake. When the war came, it was our national government that carried the whole burden. Local governments are useless in such a crisis, for unity of command is essential. To protect us from foreign invasion, to command us in our battles, and to speak for America among the nations of the world, we must look to our national government. That is the most vital service of all. Our whole safety and happiness depends upon it. For if we were a weak, divided nation, without armed forces, nor an organized government, we might be conquered, deprived of our rights, and subjected to a foreign power.

This danger of war is no remote possibility, though people are apt to forget in time of peace how constant the threat is. Our country was founded by a long and bloody war, the Revolutionary War. Since then we have fought nine wars: the War of 1812, the Mexican War, the Civil War, the Spanish-American War, World War I, World War II, the Korean War, the Vietnam War, and the Persian Gulf War. The Revolutionary War ended in 1783; the Persian Gulf War ended in 1991. That is a period of two hundred and eight years, the average interval between the wars being less than twenty-four years. The longest period between wars was from the Civil War to the Spanish-American War (1865 to 1898), which is thirty-three years. Every generation of Americans has gone to war, and every American who has lived to middle-age has lived through a war.

In time of peace, our foreign trade depends on this same force. Because our nation protects its flag wherever flown and its citizens wherever they travel, most nations respect us and allow our citizens to go where they will. If this were not so, it would be impossible for us to build up our commercial interests overseas.

The United States, as a leader of the Free World, belongs to a number of international organizations. The United Nations (U.N.) and the Organization of American States are examples of organizations that try to deal with international disputes in a peaceful manner. Originally, some form of arbitration (the settlement of a dispute between two parties) took place among the nations, and then a court of arbitration was established by treaty. A permanent court was formed in 1899, and was succeeded by the League of Nations (1920-1946) which was based on President Wilson's famed Fourteen Points of 1918.

(United Nations Photo)
The United Nations headquarters in New York.

55

One should be aware, however, that Woodrow Wilson was greatly influenced by a Fabian tract of 1917 called "Labour's War Aims." The London Fabian Society was formed in 1883, the same year Karl Marx died, and was committed to advancing socialism gradually by passing new laws. A Fabian study entitled *Labour and the New Social Order* became a sort of "Fabian Manifesto" which had four goals:

1. establishing a minimum wage and social welfare programs
2. government ownership and control of land, utilities, transportation, mineral resources, and heavy industry
3. doing away with personal property, savings, and investment through taxation
4. disarmament, an international court, international controls, and ultimately a "one-world" government.

These goals were incorporated into the League of Nations and later in the U.N. in 1945. The United Nations has consistently served the interests of socialism and globalism since 1945, and has been a bitter disappointment to those nations that yearn to be free. Most of the powerful leaders who were responsible for establishing the United Nations in the 1940s were committed to the goal of establishing a socialistic one-world government.

The International Court of Justice was established at The Hague in the Netherlands, where 15 judges from various nations meet to resolve questions of international law. It acts as an advisory or arbitrational judicial organ of the U.N.

Enemies at Home – The national government also protects us against the graver forms of disorder at home. It cannot do ordinary police work. That is left to the States, as we have seen. Your local policeman is expected to protect you against thieves, and there is an organized State militia (the National Guard) which the governor can call out to protect property and lives when there is disorder. But if a riot or a rebellion grows serious and the State authorities are unable to quell it, the State legislature (or if the legislature is not in session, the governor) is entitled to call upon the President to send troops of the national army to help (Art. IV, Sec. 4). Under the same section, it is made the duty of the national government to see that every State has "a republican form of government." This means that no State can set up a monarchy or any tyranny, and that all the troops of the United States will be called out, if necessary, to compel popular government in a State.

In one other way, the national government preserves order within the States. The President must "take care that the laws be faithfully executed" (Art. II, Sec. 3). To do this, he can use the entire army if necessary. When a strike tied up the mails in Chicago in 1894, President Cleveland sent national troops to preserve order and prevent the mails from being held up or destroyed. The mails were not stopped. In 1957, during the civil disturbances which accompanied the court-ordered racial integration at Central High School in Little Rock, Arkansas, the President called in the National Guard to quell the riots. Again in 1970, Guard troops were called in to control campus demonstrations against the war in Vietnam; and tragically, four students were killed. However, many Guard units have performed well in wartime and during natural disasters. The National Guard performs an important support role for local law enforcement officers by preventing looting and keeping the peace, like after Hurricane Andrew struck southern Florida and other Gulf States in 1992.

The Federal Bureau of Investigation (FBI), founded in 1908, is responsible for investigating any violation of federal law that is not assigned to another agency. Over 180 crimes fall under FBI jurisdiction. These include crimes such as kidnapping, bank robbery, espionage and assaults upon federal workers.

These services show how blessed we are to live in a strong, stable, unified nation, that gains us respect wherever we travel abroad and holds our lives, liberties, and property safely against riot and rebellion at home.

2. The Lesser Services

Other Services – We come now to the simpler and lesser things that the national government does for us. These have increased constantly with the growth of the country, and are likely to increase more. Why?

Our Changed Conditions – Just consider what the country was like in 1789. Then, most Americans were farmers, and each farmer produced almost everything that he and his family ate–wheat, pork, mutton, beef, milk, eggs, and so forth. His wife spun the wool and made the clothes. There were few factories. There was very little trading between States. However, the farms today are usually very large, each growing a few products which are shipped all over the country, even the world. The wheat farmer grows chiefly wheat, and so forth. Cattle are raised in the ranching States of the South and West, packed at large meat packing centers, and shipped to every city and village in the nation. In the same way, clothes are no longer made at home; they are made in factories throughout the country and are sometimes imported from other parts of the world for the whole nation. Wonderful machines have been invented for spinning and weaving, and for every other type of manufacturing process. Each factory makes one sort of thing (shoes, hats, computers, automobiles, etc.), and what it produces is shipped everywhere. To deliver all these products, railways, truck routes, and air freight systems were developed as we know them today, crossing and crisscrossing the entire country. The shipping charge is an important item in the price of almost everything we buy.

Just think, when you sit down for dinner, how many States are serving you. The wheat for your bread is grown in North Dakota, let us say, and milled in Minnesota. The steer that is now roast beef was grazed in Texas, and was killed and packed in Denver. The apples came from Oregon, the oranges from Florida. The sugar cane was grown in Louisiana and refined into sugar by way of New York; the salt was produced in Kansas. The gas that cooks the meal is from Oklahoma. The perishables, such as milk, fresh eggs, and vegetables, came from your own or a nearby state. A dozen States contribute to the simplest meal.

Take your knife and fork. If they are silver-plated, the silver was mined in Nevada, and the iron in the core of the utensil was mined in Michigan; shipped to

Pittsburgh as ore and smelted. The knife and fork were finally manufactured in Connecticut.

The leather hide used for your shoes very likely came off a Texan steer, killed in Denver. The shoes were manufactured in Massachusetts.

All this long-distance trade increases the work of the national government. When a farmer grows all his own food he knows that it is pure and healthful. Or if he buys it from a neighbor that he, knows and trusts, he can be sure. But if he has to buy meat packed in Denver or Kansas City by a stranger, he cannot possibly tell. So the government, which is to say, all of us clubbed together, sends an inspector to do this for us. If it is milk from his own State, his State government can inspect the dairies to see that the cows are healthy. But no State can act outside its own borders and most foods, as we saw, come from other states; so there is a big job here which the government in Washington alone can do.

Our vast and elaborate means of communication, the post office, the railroads, radio and television, the telephone system, and computer technology, also raise national problems which the national government has tried to handle. The government has always run the postal system, as we know. But starting a new policy, it fixed the railroad rates and began to regulate the railroads in 1887. As to whether the government can run efficiently such a complex and difficult business as our railroads, there is grave debate. Government regulation has created numerous economic problems, but many people continue to claim that such regulation is needed.

Nevertheless, America has become one large family, everybody working for everybody else, and dependent on everybody else. No one can prosper alone. What happens in one State affects the whole country. And what happens in Washington affects each State and every individual.

Therefore, we must be cautious in increasing the responsibilities and activities of our national government, for this forces the federal politicians to raise taxes to the point where our whole economy will suffer. Generally speaking, it must be remembered that governments do not and cannot create wealth, in fact they often destroy the means by which people create it. We must keep our State governments strong and use them as much as we can. When certain conditions call for new national regulation, we must routinely hesitate to give our government in Washington more power than the Constitution has already granted.

Money – A uniform system of money or currency is an essential basis of buying, selling, and commerce in a modern nation. Therefore, the States are forbidden by the Constitution to coin money (Art. I, Sec. 10, Par. 1); only the national government has the power (Art. I, Sec. 8, Par. 5). Before 1789, the States had flooded the country with paper money that, in some instances, had become worthless. Hard lessons were learned about the dangers of permitting governments to print currency that is not backed up by gold or silver in the treasury.

Sadly, during the twentieth century, our central government has voted to take our nation's currency off of a gold or silver standard. These acts are in direct violation of the U.S. Constitution (Art. I, Sec. 10, Par. 1). The dollar was taken off of the gold standard over a long period of time. In 1933, Americans were forced to turn in their gold coins and gold certificates to the Department of the Treasury. The dollar was completely removed from the gold standard in 1971, when President Nixon disallowed the converting of dollars into gold by foreign banks and governments. Later in the 1970s, the American people's right to purchase and own gold was restored, even though it is no longer designed to be used as money. Congress voted to strip our money from being backed by silver in 1964.

These actions permitted those in Congress, to spend more money on government programs without having to worry about sufficient gold or silver in the federal treasury to pay for these programs. Since the late 1960's our government has spent so much paper money trying to win the favor and votes of particular people and groups, that our nation is now burdened with a four trillion dollar debt! The people who wrote our beloved Constitution knew that it was very foolish to permit the people in our federal Congress to print paper money that was not backed up by gold or silver. This is precisely why the Constitution clearly prohibited our central government from issuing vast amounts of worthless paper money.

The people of the United States are now having to pay dearly in high taxes and an unstable economy, because they failed to stop their elected representatives from spending money in a reckless and unconstitutional manner. Uncontrolled government spending must be stopped before our nation's economy is destroyed.

The Post Office – Let us next take up the oldest of the business undertakings of the government. There were 75 post offices in 1789 in the whole country, and it cost 25 cents to send a letter more than 450 miles. For years you could send a letter from Portland, Maine, to Manila in the Philippines, over 10,000 miles, for only 21 cents. There are now over 60,000 post offices, and the average cost to mail a personal letter to some party in the United States is 32 cents.

Our post office system is one of the largest businesses in the world; but it is not run as other businesses are, to make a profit. It is run to educate, inform, and unify the nation. That is why the rates are so low and first class postage is the same wherever the Stars and Stripes are flown. It costs the government very little to deliver a newspaper to a person a few blocks away in a city. It costs the government a good deal more to deliver that same newspaper to a ranch a thousand miles away. Yet, it charges only a fraction of the larger cost of the larger haul. That is because both people are Americans and must be informed of public events and public opinion in order to be good citizens.

The post office service has grown steadily, and now includes these five things:

1.   It delivers mail from door-to-door in the large cities, as well as to remote locations over miles and miles of country roads by Rural Free Delivery.

2. It also offers General Delivery service for people who do not have a permanent address, and post office boxes located in the post office which are convenient and private.

3. It registers letters, so as to make their safe delivery more certain by insuring them and keeping careful records. Certified mail also keeps careful records but is not insured.

4. It sends money by postal orders which are like bank checks.

5. Since 1913, it has been carrying small packages by parcel-post, doing work formerly done by private companies. In recent years, many express parcel companies have come into existence which compete for business with the postal service.

Railway Rates – A large slice of what we pay for may go to the railroad that carried the items we purchase, and finally, to the place where we bought them. Think of that dinner table again. The orange from Florida, the wheat from Minnesota, the roast beef from Texas, all paid a railway charge which the grocer and butcher had to add into the price they charged you. Therefore, it is very important that railway rates should be fair, and be as low as possible without cheating the railroads.

Congress has no control over commerce on railroads wholly within one State. However, the Constitution gives Congress authority to control interstate commerce; that is, commerce between States (Art. I, Sec. 8). There was nothing but the stage coach when the Constitution was written, but the makers had the foresight to use such general and far reaching terms that it has provided for every development. Through its control of "commerce," Congress has provided for the fixing of fair and reasonable rates on all interstate traffic, freight, and passengers alike. This has been done through the Interstate Commerce Commission. This is one of the most important services that the national government has undertaken. It is another case in which the government steps in and sees that there is fair play for all – railroad, farmer, manufacturer, and consumer alike.

Panama Canal – The national government chose to build an artificial waterway in Panama for the convenience of the world's commerce, and also to give a swift passage from coast to coast for our warships; thus making the defense of our nation easier. In 1977, the United States and Panama signed a treaty which would give Panama control over the Canal by 1999.

The Nation's Health – If you will look at the meat the next time you are at your local grocery store, you will see that it is stamped "Inspected." That mark was put upon it at the packer's, in Denver, let us say, by a United States inspector. This is one of the most valuable services the government does for us. These inspectors watch every piece of meat that is packed, they condemn every piece that is diseased or unfit, and pass only the sound, wholesome meat.

This is done under the pure food and drug law passed in 1906. It applies, of course, only to interstate commerce. Under this law, drugs are required to be pure; and food must be pure and wholesome, free from poisonous and injurious substances.

Labels on food and drugs must tell the truth. Inspectors watch factories all over the country, destroy food that is spoiled, and impose fines upon manufacturers who violate the law. This important work, that means so much to the health of us all, is under the general charge of the Secretary of Agriculture.

The Farmer – The national government has done much to aid and encourage the farmer. With each new Territory added to the Union, vast, unsettled public lands have come into the ownership of the government. These have been largely given to actual settlers under the Homestead Act of 1862, which provided that any person could secure 160 acres by settling on it and cultivating it for five years. In this way, we have become a nation of landowners. (As you will recall, these public lands are in charge of the Department of the Interior.) The best of this land has now been given out, and the government has begun a series of great irrigation systems to reclaim tracts of desert and semiarid lands. Huge dams have been built and water stored in them to be distributed by canals and ditches over the dry sections. These lands are sold in small tracts to actual settlers.

The Department of Agriculture studies the farmer's problems: the breeding, feeding, and fighting of disease with respect to livestock; the improving of crops by new varieties of seeds; the testing of soils in different parts of the country, which determines the crops best suited for them; the controlling of insects and diseases which attack plants, trees, and grains; and distributing bulletins which tell what has been discovered. The Department of Commerce also helps the farmer through the National Weather Service, which warns every one, farmers included, of cold waves, frosts, and storms.

Conservation – One-quarter of the United States is still covered with forests, but it is estimated that if we go on cutting wastefully, making no provision for reforestation, our forests will eventually be entirely cut down. This shows how recklessly we have been using our natural resources, and why our new national conservation policy is so important. More than one-third of our forest acreage has been placed in reserves that are under the control of the Forest Service of the Department of Agriculture. Forest rangers patrol these acres, guarding against cutting except according to the rules of careful forestry, extinguishing fires, preventing fires by building firebreaks along the crests of ranges, and undertaking reforestation. The whole country benefits by this foresight and watchful care. The principles of conservation also include the development of our vast water power, so as to avoid a monopoly and furnish power for as many citizens as possible.

Labor – The Department of Labor studies the labor problems and labor laws of the several States and of the world, and publishes reports upon them. The regulation of labor in local factories rests chiefly with the State governments, since the national power of regulation is restricted to interstate commerce. However, independent agencies such as the National Labor Relations Board, and the Railroad Retirement Board have been established to work with the Department of Labor to regulate collective bargaining rights for workers, child labor, working conditions, minimum wages, and special rules for railroad workers.

The Protective Tariff – One of the great political issues throughout the history of the nation has been "protection." A small tariff (a customs duty) upon goods from foreign countries operates merely as a tax to produce revenue. Protection means imposing a tariff so large that foreign goods cannot be profitably imported, thus protecting American industries from foreign competition. Some have argued that the only way manufacturing could be developed and maintained is with the help of protective tariffs, because the high wages paid in America will make it impossible to produce goods as cheaply here as elsewhere. However, others have argued that the country would be better off if it could buy foreign-made goods cheaply and let manufacturing develop naturally. This disagreement was reflected in the fight over the North American Free Trade Agreement in 1993.

The Control of Trusts – One of the most serious problems in preserving fair play in American life has been raised by the growth of huge businesses called trusts or mergers. The old theory of our business life was that every bright and energetic young man could start out for himself as an independent manufacturer or dealer. Competition among these small concerns gave free play for ability to show itself and for prices to be kept down. In many respects, these conditions still exist today. But in some cases, the small concerns have all been merged into a few, and these large corporations control the field. These conditions shut out the small beginner and permit an unfair raising of prices since competition is largely ended. Such single control of any one product or service is called a monopoly.

To secure a return of fair play, both for the small business man and for the public, the nation has passed a number of laws; the chief being the Sherman Anti-trust

Law of 1890.   Under this law, great trusts, like the Standard Oil and the tobacco companies, were split up by the courts into their original small concerns. In 1914, this was supplemented by the Clayton Act, defining what "unfair trade methods" are and creating a Federal Trade Commission to enforce the law.

The problem is a very difficult one, and there has been much disagreement as to what remedy should be used. There is no question that mergers and consolidated firms can reduce costs, since they are able to buy, manufacture, and sell in larger quantities than the small manufacturer. This saving is of value to us all – provided we get the benefit of it in lower prices. Therefore, some argue that we should not compel the mega-companies to dissolve, but should regulate prices. Others believe that trusts should be split up and competition fostered by means of the laws which now prevent "unfair trade practices;" such as, selling goods far below cost to drive out a competitor, and obtaining "rebates" from railroads (that is, secret agreements for cheaper rates).

The trust or merger problem is the problem of fair play in business for the manufacturer, the laborer, and the public. It has been solved only in part, and it is doubtful that more government controls or regulations will be of any help.

The States have also passed many laws in an effort to end monopoly or prevent its evils, but with little success since their laws cannot touch interstate commerce. As long as there is greed, envy, and sin in the world, our free enterprise system will not always function perfectly. However, the free exchange of goods and services provides the best system of fair play known to mankind. It is still true that the government which governs least governs best.

Questions on the Text

1. Does the local or national government come closer to our daily life?
2. What are the greatest services that the national government does for us?
3. Why must the national government protect us from foreign enemies?
4. How many wars has America fought?
5. What was the longest period between wars and what was the average interval?
6. Of what value is it to a citizen travelling abroad to have a strong and courageous government at home?
7. What great steps have been taken toward preserving the peace of the world?
8. When does the President send troops into a State to preserve order?
9. How does the America of today differ from America of 1789?
10. Where do our foods now come from?
11. How does this change increase the responsibilities of the national government?
12. Why are the States not allowed to coin money?
13. Why is the post office not run for profit?
14. What five services does the post office offer?
15. Under what clause of the Constitution does Congress have power to regulate railroad rates?
16. Why did the nation build the Panama Canal?
17. What does the pure food and drug law provide?

18. What has the national government done for the farmer through grants of land and what is it doing now?
19. What does the Department of Agriculture do for the farmer?
20. What does conservation mean? What does the government do to preserve our forests?
21. What does the Department of Labor do for labor?
22. Why can it do no more?
23. What is a protective tariff?
24. How do some people defend this tariff? Oppose it?
25. How has it affected the nation?
26. What is a trust?
27. How can it interfere with fair play in business?
28. What is a monopoly?
29. What is the root cause of the problems our nation has with free trade and business mergers?

Questions for Discussion

1. What has the national government done for you today?
2. Has America ever been invaded?
3. Has America ever been obliged to put down a rebellion?
4. How many countries can you name that have been invaded by a foreign enemy?
5. Are foods and drugs marked in any way to show that they have been inspected by the national government?
6. Is your milk inspected by any government agency?
7. How many kinds of coins and paper money have you seen?

OUR FEDERAL GOVERNMENT NEEDS TO WAKE UP AND REALIZE THAT IT MUST STOP SPENDING MONEY THAT IT DOES NOT HAVE IN ITS TREASURY — AFTER ALL, MONEY DOES NOT GROW ON TREES!

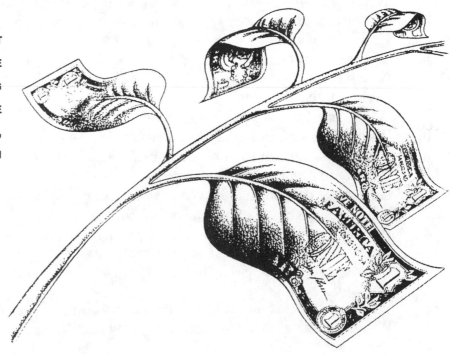

64

CHAPTER 14

The Government of a State

1. The State

State Governments – We now come to the governments of the States, including their county and municipal governments. The primary task of each State system of government has been to protect the life, liberty, and property of every citizen. The central and State governments have always had separate and specific jurisdictions, limiting the power of the federal system and allowing the States to act as a buffer between the central government and the people. As you will recall, each State is left free by the Constitution to govern itself as it sees fit in its local concerns. That is our theory of home rule. It possesses all powers not delegated to the national government and not denied to it by the Constitution (Amendment X.) Therefore, it is impossible to describe any one system of State government that will hold true of all fifty States. As a matter of fact, no two are exactly alike. What follows is only a rough sketch which must be filled in and perhaps altered a little to apply to your own State.

In general outline, the State governments are very much like the national government. The seat of the State government is the State capital. There are three branches exactly as the government in Washington, D.C.

The State Executive – The executive (corresponding to the President) is the governor, elected directly by the people of the State. His term is usually two or four years. The lieutenant-governor corresponds to the Vice-President.

One important difference to be noted is that some of the governor's chief assistants are always elected along with him by the people and not appointed by him. A treasurer and a comptroller (who handle the funds of the State), a secretary of State and an attorney-general are usually among these. (Do not confuse this secretary of State with the national Secretary of State, who has charge of our foreign affairs. The State has no foreign affairs, and its secretary is simply the keeper of the State's records and election returns.) A governor, thus, has no body of chosen advisers exactly corresponding to the President's Cabinet, and he cannot select or control his chief agents.

This feature of our State governments has been much criticized, for it divides responsibility and prevents unified handling of the State's affairs. It also puts an undue burden on the voter, who often does not know anything about the minor candidates. The "short ballot" is the name given to the plan of cutting down the number of elective offices. We have a "short ballot" in the national election now, for we vote only for President, Vice-President, senator and representative. The "short ballot" would apply the same principle to State, county, township, city, and village.

Appointments – The governor has many appointments to make. Chief among these are a superintendent of education, who has general supervision of the public schools (although some are elected by the people or appointed by the State Board of Education), a superintendent of prisons, and a State engineer, who is responsible for the State highways.

Many States have created numerous boards or commissions in recent years to handle various matters, all appointed by the governor. There are boards of agriculture, food and dairies, live stock, fish, and mining, which collect and diffuse information to promote these interests. There are boards of health, bureaus of labor and statistics, geological commissions, and forestry boards, which collect facts, conduct scientific research and (in the case of the State Board of Health) execute certain laws. There are supervising boards which regulate railroads, insurance companies, banks, etc. There are boards of examiners for those who wish to become dentists, pharmacists, barbers, etc. There are boards which have supervision of the prisons, hospitals, asylums, etc. This commission system has been much criticized for the diffusion of responsibility which it produces.

The State civil service has passed through several stages where many States have enacted civil-service reform laws to reduce the spoils system of appointment, just as the national government has.

Commander-in-Chief - The governor is Commander-in-Chief of the military forces of the State, known as the militia. All able-bodied males, ages 18 - 45, are part of either the organized or unorganized militia. For example, the Constitution of the State of Illinois declares that "the State militia consists of all able-bodied persons in the State except those exempted by law." This principle is in accord with early federal law when, in the Uniform Militia Law of 1792, Congress declared that every white male, ages 18 - 45, was subject to being called up for military service for up to three months. The primary purpose of the militia, as defined by the Constitution, is "...to execute the laws of the Union, suppress insurrections and repel invasions" (Art. I, Sec. 8, Par. 15).

The organized militia of the State has been known as the National Guard since 1878. There are both Army and Air components of the National Guard and the State could organize a Naval militia if it so desired, but no State has done so for many years. The State adjutant-general is in charge of the department that is responsible for the National Guard.

The National Guard is usually used by the governor to take care of State problems. Governors of several Midwestern States used National Guard troops to help people during the floods along the Mississippi River during 1993. The governor can also use National Guard troops to help the police contain serious outbreaks of violence. The governor of California used units of the California National Guard to help the police control the Los Angeles riots of 1992.

The militia is also an important component in our nation's defense. Militia units were called to active duty to serve in many wars, including the War of 1812, the Civil War, and all of our wars in the twentieth century. The Dick Act of 1903 declared the National Guard to be the nation's official reserve force, and the Hay Act of 1916 stated that the National Guard was subject to a federal call. The militia has also helped to enforce the laws of the nation; from enforcing federal taxes during the Whiskey Rebellion of 1794, to the use of National Guard troops to carry-out court-ordered racial integration in schools in Arkansas in 1957, and Mississippi in 1962.

The militia system is important to preserve. It prevents the central government from usurping the State's rights, freedom, and sovereignty. The Second Amendment to the Constitution ("A well-regulated militia, being necessary to the security of a free State, the right of the people to keep and bear arms, shall not be infringed.") supports the militia system by both guaranteeing that the State keeps a militia, and keeping the power of the militia in the hands of the people by recognizing their right to own weapons which can be used to protect themselves, the State, and the nation from tyranny.

Pardons – The governor has a pardoning power like the President's, but it is usually restricted. In many States, a board of pardons is provided which either hears pleas for pardon and makes recommendations to the governor, or passes finally on all pardons, and must approve before they take effect. Included in the right of pardon is the power to grant a reprieve (that is, a stay of the execution of a sentence, the death penalty, for instance) pending investigation or some other legal step, and the power to commute a sentence, that is, change it to a lesser sentence. The President's pardoning power includes these same features, but it is not as important, since the control of most crimes rests with the States.

Legislative Powers – These are like the legislative powers of the President. He can call the legislature in special session in an emergency, he sends messages to the the legislature, and he can veto bills (in every State except North Carolina). The legislature can pass a bill over his veto by a two-thirds vote in some States, a three-fifths vote in others, or in a few States by a bare majority.

The State Legislature - The legislatures of most states have two houses contrasting in size and length of term very much, as do the House and Senate in Washington, D.C. The larger body is called the House of Representatives, Assembly, or House of Delegates. The smaller body is called the Senate. The only exception is the State of Nebraska, which has only one legislative body. State legislators are elected by districts, and for this purpose each State is divided into two sets of districts; larger ones for senators, smaller ones for representatives. Districts are usually arranged on the basis of population so that each senator represents about the same number of inhabitants, and each representative represents about the same number. The houses are organized and bills are introduced and passed very much as in Washington, D.C.

The State Constitution and Courts – There is a State constitution exactly as there is a national Constitution; and there are State courts (including a supreme court sitting at the capital) to interpret the State laws and the State constitution. The State constitution contains a Bill of Rights protecting the freedom of the people, their religious liberty, their right of free speech, exactly as does the national constitution. Your State constitution is the highest law of the State, just as the national Constitution is the highest law of the nation. It is a most important protection of the people's rights, for it restrains the State legislature from interfering with your freedom, just as the national Constitution restrains Congress.

The national Constitution is, of course, binding on the State legislature, just as it is binding on everybody else. But by a curious omission, it does not protect religious liberty, the right of free speech, or personal liberty against State laws. This is not a serious matter since all the State constitutions fully protect these rights and always have protected them. It was because the State constitutions already contained these Bills of Rights in 1787, that the national Constitution was originally designed not to cover these points.

The powers of each State are very wide, as we have seen (and shall examine in detail in the next chapter). But the powers of State legislatures have been much limited by means of detailed provisions in the State constitutions. That is to say, the people of the individual States have not trusted their legislatures with the same freedom that the people of the whole country have trusted Congress. There is usually a debt limit beyond which the State legislature cannot go, and limits to taxation are often fixed. In some States, the legislature is limited by constitutional restrictions upon almost every subject. One result of this condition is that our State constitutions are very long and confusing by comparison with our national Constitution. However, this is a small price to pay for keeping state law makers from exceeding their just and lawful authority.

Amendments – State constitutions require frequent amendment, owing to the large amount of detailed legislation in them. They can be amended in two ways, as a rule: (1) by a constitutional convention called by the legislature, in which case an entirely new constitution may be drafted; whatever the convention adopts, it must be submitted to the voters and takes effect only if it is ratified by them; and (2) the State legislature itself can propose amendments. In some States, a two-thirds vote is required. In others, the amendment must be passed by a legislature in two different years. In all States, the proposed amendment must be submitted to the voters exactly as after a constitutional convention. A third method is permitted: A certain small percentage of the voters can petition for an amendment, in which case it is submitted to popular vote without coming before either convention or legislature. This use of the "initiative," as it is called, will be discussed again in connection with elections in Chapter 17.

The State Courts – These are necessarily much more numerous and complex than the federal courts, for they handle many more cases since the State laws control most of the common affairs of life. The titles and organizations vary in the different States, the general plan is as follows:

1. Justice of the peace. Elected by the town. (In cities, police magistrates try the same cases.)
2. County judge. Elected by the county.
3. Superior, district, or circuit court. Elected by districts (each usually including several counties) in most States, but appointed by the governor in some States and elected by the State legislature in others.
4. Supreme court or court of appeals. Elected by the people of the State in most States, but appointed by the governor in some States and elected by the State legislature in others.

The justice of the peace tries small crimes and civil suits for small sums, up to $100 or $200 as a rule.

The county judge tries cases of more importance, civil suits up to a limit usually of a few thousand dollars, and almost all criminal trials. He also has charge of the important matters of wills (by which property is left at death), and the guardianship of children whose parents have died. For these reasons, he is sometimes called the probate court (for the "proving" of wills) or judge of the orphan's court. Sometimes there is a separate court for these latter purposes. "Surrogate" is another name for the judge having charge of those matters relating to the property of the dead.

The trial of all other cases, civil and criminal, comes before the superior, district, or circuit court as it is variously called.

The supreme court or court of appeals hears only appeals from the lower courts. It does not try cases; it only settles doubtful questions of law that have arisen in trials. It sits at the State capital and is a court of great importance and distinction. The only court above it is the Supreme Court of the United States. Appeals can be taken from a State supreme court to the national Supreme Court when, and only when, a question involving the national Constitution arises. In all other cases the decision of the State supreme court is final. It is, therefore, the final interpreter of the State laws and State constitution.

States are Not Nations – Each State is thus governed very much as if it were a little nation. But you already know why it is not really a nation at all. Its power to govern itself is strictly limited to local affairs, building roads, punishing murder, and so on, within its own borders. It cannot do the things that a real nation can do. It cannot make war; it cannot impose a tariff against a foreign country or between States; it cannot coin money; it cannot make a treaty with a foreign nation. (These restrictions upon the States are contained in Art. I, Sec. 10 of the Constitution.) It yielded up all these national rights in entering the Union - that is, in becoming part of one united nation.

Our Double Government – This idea of double government, of fifty State governments all under one federal government, seems confusing at first. But it works without serious confusion, since each government has its own job assigned to it and must stick to that job. It is as simple as the case of the postman and the policeman discussed before. Both walk the same street and serve the same houses without any conflict; yet one takes his orders and is paid from Washington, the other from the city or village he serves.

2. County and Town

County and Town – Local self-government is an important part of America's heritage, and is based on the Biblical teaching that every citizen is responsible for his or her actions before God. The county and municipal governments are the primary means by which local government gives power to the individual to carry out the God-ordained responsibilities that each citizen is endowed with. Each State subdivides itself into a number of small districts, and gives these districts a large measure of home rule. No two States handle this problem alike and, of course, a State can change the system of local government whenever it pleases. That is entirely within its own control. All States are divided into counties (except Louisiana, which has "parishes"). These counties are divided again into smaller districts called by various names, but usually towns or townships. Also, in all States where a number of people live close together, that is, in a village or a city, they are permitted to govern themselves as a separate unit, known as a municipality.

There are three main types of local government, the "town" system of New England, the "county" system of the South and the Far West, and the "township" system of the Middle West.

The Town System – This grew up around the New England meeting-house or church. Once a year, the voters go in person to a "town meeting," now held in a "town hall." Here they discuss the needs of the community, fix the tax rate, pass by-laws (that is to say, town laws, for "by" is an old English word meaning town), and elect town officers. These latter include a board of three to nine "selectmen" who have general charge of the business of the town: a clerk (who keeps the town records), a tax assessor, a treasurer, an overseer of public health and welfare, a school committee, a police chief, and a surveyor of highways (who keeps roads in repair). There are many other minor officials. Two or three other town meetings are usually held in the course of a year, at which other town business is discussed and settled.

Do not misunderstand this use of the word "town" in New England. It does not mean a city or a village as it does elsewhere. A New England town usually includes a village; but it includes the surrounding farms as well, an area of perhaps four or five square miles, with an average of 3,000 inhabitants.

The town meeting exists chiefly in New England (although parts of Illinois, Michigan, Wisconsin, and Minnesota still use it). Elsewhere, voters elect their officers by ballot on Election Day, and never gather in a meeting. You can see that the New England system is best suited to a small and compact community.

In this system the town was the original unit, and has remained the important unit; and the county, appearing later, has much less to do than elsewhere. It is merely a group of towns with a county-seat, at which sit county judges (with a sheriff to carry out their judgments, make arrests, etc.), and county commissioners whose chief business is the care of highways.

The County System – There are smaller divisions than the county in the Southern States, bearing various names, but they have little importance. Practically all the governing is done by the county officers. This system arose in the South, because the sparseness of the population made local self-government impracticable. But generally, the county controls everything. It also prevails in Colorado, Wyoming, Montana, Idaho, Nevada, California, Oregon, and Washington. In some of these States, local districts known as precincts, or townships elect justices of the peace and other minor officers.

The government usually consists of a board of county commissioners, a treasurer, a superintendent of education, a superintendent of public health and welfare, and an overseer of roads. There are also county judges, a county prosecutor or State's attorney, a sheriff, and a coroner (who investigates mysterious deaths). The county-seat is an important spot, since it contains the county court house, the county jail, and all the county records. The board of commissioners has much power in this system. It has entire charge of the business of the county, including the erection of county buildings, the levying of taxes, the making of appropriations, the building and repair of roads, and the care of the poor.

The sheriff is an extremely important officer. Aided by his deputy sheriffs, he is responsible for the peace of the whole county, and he carries out the orders of the county court. If property is ordered sold to make payment for a binding judgment, the sheriff does the work. If need be to maintain order or hunt down a criminal, he can call to his aid every able-bodied man in the county, forming what is called a *posse comitatus*. All prisoners are in his custody and he usually has charge of the county jail. The county clerk has charge of the records of the county. All deeds, or legal transfers of property, are recorded either with him or with a register of deeds. In the South, the schools are usually in charge of a county school board with full power to establish and run schools.

The county government gives the people the greatest amount of power in the nation. Since the county is created by and for administering the benefits of the State government, it is actually a subdivision of a particular State. Though county government varies throughout the nation, it does have the following legal functions:

1. To assess and collect taxes
2. To pass local ordinances
3. To build and maintain local roads
4. To enforce essential health and safety standards
5. To oversee and manage local and national elections
6. To register and keep public or legal records
7. To maintain police and fire departments
8. To administer justice through State and county courts

There are three notable omissions from this list: 1) public education, which belongs under the authority of the family, 2) welfare, which rightfully belongs under the control of the family and the local church, and 3) the utilities, which belong in the hands of private enterprise. Sadly, these three areas of responsibility are commonly being given to county and State governments with a resulting loss in authority for parents and other private citizens. As Americans continue to hand over more and more responsibilities to the State, and ultimately to the federal government, we will see our rights and liberties usurped.

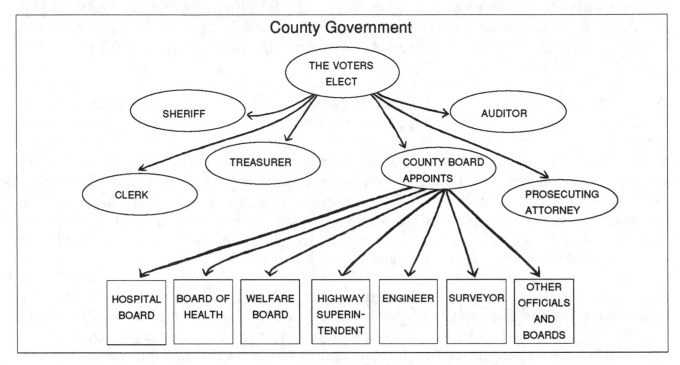

The Township System – This is sometimes called the "mixed system," since it combines features of both town and county systems. In most of these States, the county appeared first, and the townships came later as the population grew more dense; but the township has never gained the importance of the New England town. It prevails in the Middle Atlantic States and the Middle West. In the West the township is a product of the original government survey which mapped out the land in regular plots six miles square, and called these "townships." In these States, the local township governments usually developed around the schoolhouse, just as the New England town had developed around the church.

There are two general types, that of New York (in which the township rivals the county in importance) and that of Pennsylvania (in which the county is the all important unit). As the nation developed to the west, settlers generally followed lines of latitude: roughly speaking, many of the most northerly States followed the example of New York (Michigan, Wisconsin, Nebraska, for example); on the other hand, the States through the central Midwest (Ohio, Indiana, Iowa, Missouri, and Kansas) followed the example of Pennsylvania. In Illinois a division took place, the southern part preferring the county plan of Pennsylvania, and the northern part choosing the New York township system. The State constitution gives each county its choice; and under this provision 84 counties have adopted the township system of government.

In the New York type, the town meeting is usually preserved, but is not largely attended. The county board is composed of supervisors, one elected by each township. In the Pennsylvania type, there are no town meetings and the county board consists of commissioners elected by the whole county.

The county, wherever the township system prevails, always has its county judges, prosecuting attorney, sheriff, and coroner. It also has a county clerk (and, sometimes, a register of deeds), a treasurer, a superintendent or commissioner of schools (whose powers are supervisory), a superintendent of highways, and a superintendent of public health and welfare; but these positions may vary or not exist in all areas of the country.

Under the township system, the schools may be run by the school directors or trustees of the township. But more often, each township is divided into several school districts, and each of these districts elects a board called by various names (school committee, school trustees, board of education, etc.), which has full charge of the school, including the right to raise money by taxes, to hire teachers, and to build schools. This election sometimes takes place as part of the general township election and sometimes is held at an annual school meeting of parents and taxpayers, resembling a New England town meeting.

The township commonly has the following officers: one, two, or three supervisors (who have charge of the roads, etc.), a clerk, tax assessors, a tax collector, director of public welfare, school directors or trustees, justices of the peace (who try minor cases), and in rare cases, police officers.

You see how varied the methods are of local government. Each State works out its own plan suited to its own conditions. The thickly settled State can turn local affairs over to small units; the sparsely settled State can organize itself through larger units. Every local condition of the county or town can be considered and met.

3. Village and City

Village and City – When people live closely together, all kinds of things must be done by the community which rural districts leave to the individual. Sidewalks must be paved, streets must be lit, sewers must be laid, water must be supplied in pipes from a safe source (for in a congested area, wells can collect germs and spread disease); the danger of a fire spreading is much greater, so there must be an efficient fire department; burglars often invade villages and cities, so there must be a strong police force; traffic must be regulated; contagious diseases very carefully watched to prevent their spread, and so on.

Now, the county or the town could, of course, handle all these matters for the village or the city. But that is not the American way. Since the village and the city have their own special problems, the State gives them their own governments. The granting of this right is called a charter. It organizes the village or city government, known as a municipality; just as a constitution does the State or national governments. Municipalities are formed by the initiative of the people in a certain area who want to create a city or village. This is based on the freedom of movement, which is a right of the people to live and work wherever they choose. This freedom of choice in where a family prefers to settle is unfortunately being infringed upon by the zoning laws and various laws of land use. The people, originally, had the power of land use and zoning under the Common Law. But this power is now being turned over to zoning boards and the civil government, so we are beginning to be told where we can and cannot live!

Village and city are much alike, except that the city government is more complicated and has, of course, much more to do. In some parts of the United States villages are called boroughs or towns.

City Government –A city elects a mayor and a city council, or board of aldermen, usually elected by wards which are districts or divisions of a city. The aldermen are really a little legislature having power to pass what are called city ordinances; that is, local rules like requiring householders to clear their sidewalks of snow, requiring houses to be built of fireproof materials, and so forth. The city council also raises money by taxes and directs how it shall be spent - for parks, streets, schools, etc. (In a few cities, the city council consists of two houses as in a State legislature.)

The mayor of a great city like New York, Chicago, or Los Angeles is a very important and powerful officer. He is the chief executive, corresponding to the President and the governor. He usually appoints all the heads of departments, that is to say, commissioners having charge of these matters:

Police   Housing
Fire   Schools
Health   Utilities (water, gas, and electricity)
Streets and Sanitation   Taxes
Parks

The mayor also has a veto power over the acts passed by the board of aldermen. There is great variety in the city governments, but the general outline is usually as above. The city has a number of important courts, in particular the police courts, which deal with drunkenness and other small crimes. In many cities, juvenile courts have now been created to give special care to children arrested and accused of crime.

The State delegates certain powers to the local municipality through the legal process of incorporation. This process solves any problems of responsibility and liability in the case of litigation that is directed against the city. Incorporation gives the local government the same rights that an individual has, such as ownership of property, making contractual agreements, and the ability to take legal action. Therefore, a municipality can function within its jurisdiction and also protect itself by lawful means. As an individual is responsible and liable for his or her actions, so a city can spread the corporate burden over its many members.

Commission Government – Many cities have abandoned the foregoing system and are using a "commission government." A small board, usually of five members, is elected, and the entire business of governing the city is turned over to it. The object is to unify control and responsibility. This system originated in Galveston, Texas, after the great flood of 1900. The commission acts as both executive and legislature.

A city manager is sometimes used under this plan. He is an expert, to whom the commission turns over the executive work very much as if the city were a business undertaking. The commission keeps its legislative powers. In choosing a city manager, the commission can search the country over for the best expert it can find. It is hoped to develop city managers as able as the heads of our great private corporations.

Where the commission system is used, it is customary to give the voters a direct voice in lawmaking by devices known as the "initiative" and "referendum." These will be explained in detail later on in the text.

Village Government – A village elects a president, a board of trustees or councilmen, a collector of taxes, and a treasurer. These meet regularly and transact all the business of the village, including the fixing of tax rates and the passing of village ordinances. They are executive and legislature combined.

There is usually no village court, the local judge being the justice of the peace, who is chosen for a town or township.

The village board of trustees does not have charge of the local public schools, it should be noted. These are in charge of officers chosen by the school district or town or township as described before. (This is unlike the city, which does run its schools.)

Questions on the Text

Section 1

1. Does the State government resemble the national government in general outline?
2. Who is the executive of a State?
3. Are his chief assistants appointed or elected?
4. Name some of them.
5. What objection is there to this system and what change has been proposed?
6. Who commands the State militia and what is its use in peace and in war?
7. What pardoning power has the governor?
8. What is a reprieve?
9. What is a commutation of sentence?
10. What are the principal appointees of a governor?
11. What boards or commissions do States have?
12. What legislative power has the governor?
13. Describe a State legislature and tell how its members are elected.
14. How often do State legislatures meet and how do they do business?
15. Why are the State constitutions important to all of us?

16. Why have the State constitutions become lengthy and why do they require frequent amendment?
17. How are they amended?
18. Describe the courts of a State and explain how the highest court is the final interpreter of the State constitution.
19. Why are the States not nations?
20. Describe the double government we are under.

Section 2

21. How is a State divided?
22. Describe the town system of New England.
23. Describe the county system of the Southern and far Western States.
24. Who are the chief officers under the county system?
25. Describe the township system in New York and in Pennsylvania.
26. Who are the chief officers of a township?

Section 3

27. Why do villages and cities require special governments of their own?
28. What is a charter?
29. Who is the executive of a city?
30. What is its legislature like, what sort of laws can it pass, and what other powers does it have?
31. How many city commissioners can you name?
32. What two distinct types of courts does a city have?
33. What is a commission government of cities?
34. What officers has a village government?
35. Who is the local judge for small cases in a village or town?

Questions for Discussion

1. Where is your State capital?
2. Who is your governor?
3. What is this term and salary?
4. What other officers are elected?
5. What important appointments does the governor make?
6. Have you a State militia?
7. What State boards or commissions has your State?
8. What vote is required in the legislature to pass a bill over the governor's veto?
9. What are names of the two houses of your State legislature?
10. How many members in each, when elected, for what terms, and what are their salaries?
11. How often does your legislature sit?
12. Do you know how long your State constitution is and how often it is amended?
13. How can your State constitution be amended?
14. Give as many illustrations of our double government (like the policeman and postman) as you can.

15. How many counties are there in your State?
16. What is the name of your county and where is the county seat?
17. Do you live in a town, a township, or some other subdivision of a county?
18. What is its name?
19. How many of these subdivisions are there in your county?
20. What are the county officers and do you know the names of any occupants of these offices?
21. Draw a map showing your home, your school, village or city, church, police station, and county, with the county seat.

Number of Counties: 102

Map of Illinois

Showing present counties and county seats

Test 5

CHAPTER 15

What the State Does for Us

1. Through State Officials

State Government Important – American voters sometimes pay little interest to the election of their State officers, but they are really most important. They touch the daily life of every one of us, both directly and also through the fact that State laws create and control our local governments.

Voting – Each State has full power to say which of its citizens shall vote, which is part of the home rule policy of our Constitution. The only restriction is that of the Fifteenth Amendment, passed to secure the vote for all citizens after the days of slavery; which declares that "the right of citizens of the United States to vote shall not be denied or abridged by the United States or by any State on account of race, color, or previous condition of servitude."

Laws of Person and Property – It is the State that makes almost all of the laws affecting our persons and properties, which is of the utmost importance to every man, woman, and child. The law of marriage and divorce, who may marry and for what causes they may separate, is decided by each State. The State laws define all the common crimes (murder, robbery, etc.) and fix the sentence for each crime. The State builds and maintains the jails for these punishments. All the rights of property (how land may be bought and sold, what contracts must be in writing, and so on) are for the State legislatures to decide. The forest, fish, and game laws, stating at what seasons wild animals can be taken or shot, are State laws (except in the national parks, of course). This produces some confusion, because the laws of any two States are not alike. But it enables each State to pass the kind of laws best suited to its people and mode of life, and that is a great advantage.

Health – The State government maintains our asylums for the insane, the deaf, dumb, and blind. (Most hospitals are not State institutions, but are run by public-spirited citizens and supported largely by gifts.) Many States have pure food and drug laws like the national law already described.

Education – The State has a commissioner of education who has general charge of the public schools. The general courses of study and examinations to be passed by each grade are often fixed by this State authority. The State university system is supported by State funds, where students can study such things as the liberal arts, agricultural sciences, engineering, law, and education. The State has not been given the power to control private education under the Constitution. However, certain States have proceeded to pass regulations that force private schools to adopt the standards of government schools. In recent years, many State courts have begun to limit the States ability to control its "competition" in the private and home school sector. These court decisions recognize the fact that burdensome State control over private education violates the Constitutional rights of parents and school administrators.

Labor – The State will often pass laws that attempt to make our factories safe, and laws that prevent children under fourteen from working, as well as similar laws. Inspectors check businesses to enforce these laws, seeing that dangerous machinery is safeguarded, that crowded buildings have fire-escapes, that there is sufficient fresh air, and that other rules are complied with. At times, these regualtions can be enforced so strictly that private industry cannot function effectively or profitably.

Workmen's compensation laws usually provide that a workman injured through his work must be paid by his employer a certain fixed sum, graded according to the amount of the injury; or if he is killed, a fixed sum paid to his family. Such laws thus parallel the national workmen's compensation act; but the national act benefits only workers on interstate railroads, whereas State laws can protect every worker injured within the State.

State Highways – Prior to the twentieth century, all roads were built by the town or county; but starting in the 1920's, many States have undertaken the building of important highways, forming through routes. The growth of the automobile industry has prompted the development of many State highways.

2. Through the City

The City – The closer people live together, the more they must do in common, that is, through their government; in order that they may live safely and comfortably. Therefore, a large city does a great many more things than a village; and a village more things than a town, township, or county for its rural districts. There must be more rules and regulations in a city – traffic rules, for instance, which are quite unnecessary in the country. If we take up city life first, we can then compare it with village and rural life to see how they differ.

The Police Department – Service in the police department is like service in the army. A policeman always goes armed, with a handgun and a night-stick. He wears a uniform, unless he is working undercover and needs to hide his identity to learn more about certain criminals. The chief differences are that he fights not an army but one or a few criminals at a time, and that he fights usually alone. Every policeman risks his life in serving us.

The policeman is the enemy of every law-breaker and the friend of every honest person. The traffic policeman helps little children cross a crowded street. Mounted policemen stop runaway thieves. Finding lost children and returning them to their homes is a frequent duty. Many policemen have rescued men, women, and children from burning buildings. All this help is as much a part of their duty as their work of watching for criminals night and day, and arresting them whenever they break the law. The main job of the local police is to help maintain the peace and order of the city they serve.

It is the duty of every citizen, man, boy, woman and girl, to help a policeman whenever possible. That is the law, and it is common sense as well, for the policeman

is our policeman. It is our laws that he is enforcing, our property that he is protecting, our lives that he may save. Boys and girls should know the policeman in their neighborhood and help him. He is one of the best friends that they have, and they may owe their life to him some day when their house catches fire or a robber seeks to steal their money.

Every police force usually includes a squad of detectives in plain clothes (therefore often called "plain-clothes men"). At police headquarters, a type of rogues' gallery, is maintained which contains photographs and physical descriptions of many criminals. In 1879, a complex system of accurate measurements of the head and other parts of the body was invented by a Frenchman named Alphonse Bertillon. By this system, an arrested criminal who gave false identification was identified at once, and his whole record would be produced against him. However, this system was supplanted in the late 1890's by the present fingerprint method.

The police department is run either by one man, called a chief of police, or by a board of police commissioners. In either case, they are appointed by the mayor. The main office is called police headquarters. The city is divided into precincts, each with a police station under the control of a captain or chief.

The Fire Department – Our firemen fight a war that never ends. At any hour of the day or night, they must be ready to come to our rescue. The risk to their lives is even greater than that of policemen. They are everyday heroes, quite as brave and daring as any soldiers.

The growth of tall buildings has made fire fighting in cities much more difficult than it was, but inventions have kept pace with the difficulties. Water towers, extension ladders, and helicopters with water containers are now familiar sights. If there are navigable waters about a city (as at New York), fireboats lend great aid.

Volunteer firemen once ran the fire apparatus of the cities, as they still do in some of our villages. But they have now given way to trained firemen paid by the city they serve.

Every boy and girl can (1) help to prevent fires, and (2) send in an alarm instantly if he or she discovers a fire.

Fire prevention is now taught to every one, old and young, in every large city. Refuse is cleaned up and carted away to prevent spontaneous combustion (that is, fire that starts itself in greasy rags and other flammable substances). Every one is taught not to throw away lighted matches or lighted cigarettes or cigars. Every one is taught the very great care required in handling alcohol, kerosene, and gasoline. Gasoline is particularly dangerous, for it is a high explosive that can burst into flames when its fumes come into contact with a tiny spark.

Never try to put out a fire yourself until you have sent in an alarm. Every boy and girl ought to know where the nearest fire-alarm is, and how to open it and pull down the hook. If you have a telephone in the house, call "911", which is the quickest way to report a fire. After you have sent in the alarm, you can try to put out the fire. Any number of fires have gained dangerous headway because people waited to send in an alarm until after they had tried to put out the fire – and failed.

The fire department is run by a fire commissioner who is appointed by the mayor.

Public Health – The progressive city does any number of things to preserve and better the health of its citizens. The growth of medical science has taught us that the germs of disease threaten us in foul air, in impure food, in street dust, and in dirt of every kind. Every person must keep clean to avoid sickness, and every home must be kept clean. Beyond this personal cleanliness, no one can do much in a great city to make sure of protection against germs. No one can keep all the streets clean. So the community attends to these jobs for each of us.

The city's health department (headed by a health commissioner, appointed by the mayor) inspects food supplies, working with the national and State inspectors to protect the consumer from injurious foods. Most important of all is the milk supply, which usually comes from within the State. Impure milk causes the death of babies and spreads many diseases. Milk inspectors not only test the milk when it arrives, but inspect the dairies to see that only healthy cows are in the herds, and that clean methods prevail.

The health department also prevents the spread of infectious diseases by quarantining every one who comes down with such a disease. Every doctor is required to report all infectious cases at once. Thereupon, the health board officer posts notices of the quarantine and sees that it is enforced. It is the duty of every one to obey such a quarantine, for otherwise the most deadly diseases would spread throughout a city.

The street cleaning commissioner not only makes city streets tidy, but prevents disease as well. By sweeping streets, flushing them with water, and removing garbage and waste in closed trucks to prevent dust from blowing about. The street cleaning department can contribute much to the health of a city, as well as, to its sightliness. It is every one's duty to help in this work by not throwing paper or refuse in the street.

Fresh air is the greatest enemy of germs, therefore, schoolrooms must be well ventilated. The city does much to secure us fresh air through two departments. The park commissioner has charge of the parks, and in a properly laid out city there are ample parks to offer breathing space in every crowded section. The building and zoning commissioner enforces rules requiring that every tenement shall have at least a certain amount of air space and a certain number of windows. The city also sees that there are enough stairways and fire escapes to save every one in case of fire. Factories are usually inspected and made safe and healthful by State inspectors, but city inspectors often do this work, too.

Recreation – Closely akin to these health measures are playgrounds for children, public beaches, public swimming pools, and other sources of recreation. Everything that keeps people out in the open aids their health, so many cities expend large sums of money to enable the inhabitants to play out-of-doors. These matters are usually in charge of the park commissioner.

Many cities also run their own public libraries, in an attempt to encourage people of every age to stay well informed and educated.

Streets – The paving and upkeep of streets is a very important part of a city's service. Well-paved streets do more than anything else to make a city pleasant place to live. A commissioner of public works usually has charge of these matters.

Water, Gas, Electricity, Transportation Systems – Most cities run their own water-works and mass transit systems. Many towns also run their gas and electric plants. For all these services, the city charges rates just like a private company. When it does not own these services, the rates charged are regulated by commissions. Services of this kind are called public utilities, which simply means things of use to the public generally. It is the theory, nowadays, that private owners of such services must submit to reasonable regulation by the government for the good of all. Whether a city shall own and run its transportation system parallels the question explained before, whether the national government shall own and run the interstate railways of the whole country. There are strong arguments on both sides.

3. Through the Village

The Village – The progressive village does almost all of the things that the city does, but in a simpler way and on a much smaller scale. There is usually a chief of police and a small police force. The fire department is usually a volunteer organization, but it is often very efficient, and many villages now have several fire engines. A health officer does not have as much to do, but his control of infectious diseases is important in preventing epidemics. Libraries in villages can be just as good as those in large cities.

4. In Rural Districts

Rural Districts — Farmers and other American citizens who live in the rural areas of our country look to their local township or county government for police protection. The town deputies are the regular police officers, but in case of any serious crime or disturbance, the county sheriff and his deputy sheriffs step in. Some States have a State police force whose duty it is to patrol rural districts and main highways.

The roads—other than State or Federal highways—are built and repaired by the supervisors of the town or township; or, as in the case of the State of Virginia, by the county commissioners.

Individuals who live in rural areas very often are unable to take advantage of services which are available to city dwellers. Most of the needs that confront rural Americans—such as fire protection, proper sanitation, and clean water—must be dealt with by the local citizens themselves. This situation requires people in rural areas to be more self-reliant and to solve their own problems, and to work with their neighbors to take care of local community needs. Rural fire protection shows this tendency, as citizens often join together to form volunteer fire-departments to protect their communities.

All citizens who are interested in promoting the true American way of life must try to resist the temptation to let big government solve the problems of local communities and rural areas. May God help all Americans to provide for themselves and their families, as much as possible, without shifting their responsibilities to governmental agencies.

Questions on the Text

Section 1

1. Why are the services of the State important to every one?
2. What government determines who shall vote?
3. How does the Fifteenth Amendment affect this power?
4. What government has the power to pass laws touching our persons and property?
5. Name as many of these laws of persons and property as you can.
6. Even though confusion may result from having various States passing different laws on these subjects, what good comes from it?
7. What health measures does the State undertake?
8. What are the duties of the commissioner of education?
9. Why is it dangerous for the State to control private schools?

Section 2

10. Why are there more rules in a city and why must there be more public services?
11. Name all the duties of a policeman that you can.
12. What is the rogues' gallery?
13. Who is the head of the police department?
14. What can we do to prevent fires?
15. What must we do the instant we discover a fire?
16. Do you know how to send in an alarm?
17. Describe the two chief branches of the health department's service.
18. How does the street-cleaning commissioner aid public health?
19. Why should we have abundant parks?
20. What do the building or zoning inspectors do?
21. What recreations do cities furnish?
22. What are public utilities?

Section 3

23. How does village government differ from city government?

Section 4

24. To what government and what officers does a farmer look for police protection?
25. What officers have the care of rural roads?

Questions for Discussion

1. Are there any State institutions near your home?
2. Do you know where the State university and colleges are located?
3. How much control does your State commissioner of education exert over your school and your courses of study?
4. Have you ever seen a factory law posted in a factory and do you know any factory regulations?
5. What is the child labor law of your State?
6. Has your State a workmen's compensation law?
7. Are there any State highways near your home?
8. What public utilities does your city or village own or run?
9. Are your local roads good or bad?
10. What does self-government mean?

THE ILLINOIS STATE BUDGET

APPROPRIATIONS

In Fiscal Year 1993, total state appropriations are estimated at $29.1 billion, including $13.2 billion in general funds.

Approximately one-fourth of the state's budget is spent on education. More than $4.2 billion is appropriated for elementary and secondary education, while higher education appropriations will exceed $2.7 billion.

The Department of Public Aid, with $6.4 billion for its medical assistance, income assistance and other social service programs, is the largest agency in terms of appropriations. The Department of Transportation, due to the multi-year nature of its programs, is next largest with $4.7 billion.

The Health and Human Services component of the state budget, comprised of the Departments on Aging, Alcoholism and Substance Abuse, Children and Family Services and Mental Health and Developmental Disabilities, among others, totals about $3.2 billion. The remaining $7.9 billion supports all other governmental activities, including debt repayment, law enforcement, revenue collection, elected officials and the Legislative and Judicial Branches of State Government.

APPROPRIATIONS BY MAJOR PURPOSE — FY 1993 — Percent of Total

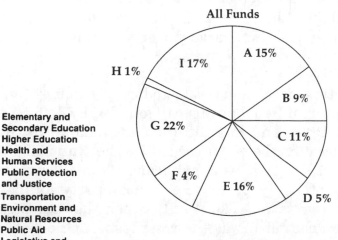

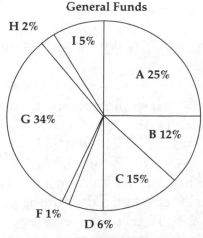

A Elementary and Secondary Education
B Higher Education
C Health and Human Services
D Public Protection and Justice
E Transportation
F Environment and Natural Resources
G Public Aid
H Legislative and Judicial
I All Other

CHAPTER 16

Political Parties and Elections

1. A Sacred Duty

The Ballot – We come now to the most important civic duty of an American, the basis of all the fine structure we have studied. That is to vote, wisely and patriotically. A certain number of Americans always fail to turn up on Election Day. They are too lazy or too indifferent. They are cheating themselves out of their birthright, that should be their proudest possession; they are cheating their country, for they enjoy her protection and care, and they refuse to bear the chief responsibility of citizenship. There is no magic in the word "republic." Unless the citizens of a country give it their best wisdom and aid whenever needed, it will become corrupt, and perish.

2. Parties

The Reason for Parties – You must understand political parties in order to understand elections. There is nothing about them in the Constitution. They have grown up gradually to satisfy a natural tendency in human nature, that is, to unite in groups to support certain ideas and certain leaders. Sometimes a great leader creates an idea and the party forms around him. Sometimes the idea is developed by a party, and the leader is merely chosen to carry the idea into effect. Whichever way it happens, most people instinctively join such a group. We call those who prefer to remain out of the party system, "independents." They are a small but important part of any community.

The Two Main Parties – There have usually been two main parties in the United States. Under changing names, they have lasted down to our present time. In the first years of the republic, the two parties were the Federalist (the party of Hamilton and John Adams) and the Democratic-Republican, usually called simply Republican (the party of Jefferson). The former believed in a broad construction of the Constitution, giving the national government wide powers. The latter believed in a strict construction, and in holding the national government to the powers clearly set forth in the Constitution. The dispute was largely over the "elastic clause" referred to before (Art. I, Sec. 8, Par. 18).

In a very general way, this distinction has lasted right through: only the names have become reversed. The original Republican party founded by Jefferson changed its name to Democratic about 1828, and has retained that name to this day. The Federalists lasted only a generation, being succeeded by the National Republicans of 1828, the Whigs from 1833 to 1854, and the Republicans of 1854 down to the present. New issues have arisen frequently. The present Republican party sprang up to oppose slavery and advocate a protective tariff. The War Between the States ended slavery, and after that for many years the tariff was the chief issue. Of course, many other issues have, from time to time, come to the front; and by the early 1920's, the issues had become much confused. But the original dispute over the strength of the national government still persists in the same degree to distinguish the two parties.

Third Parties – Third parties have sprung up from time to time, as a new group appeared around a new idea or a new leader not acceptable to either of the old parties. (That was the way the new Republican party began in 1854.) Most of these parties died out after a few years. Of this type were the Populist party, a farmer's party formed in 1892, and the Progressive party, formed in 1912 to advocate new policies under the leadership of Theodore Roosevelt. The Socialist party is a third party which has slowly gained in strength and maintained its existence without electing many officials. In recent years, third parties have arisen over ownership of business and natural resources, civil and States' rights, as well as economic matters.

Independent Voting – Every voter must keep his mind alive to these changes, study the new problems as they arise, and decide whether or not he wishes to join a new party and how it seems wisest to cast his vote. No country can stand still. It must go ahead or fall behind. No voter does his duty who sits back and votes with his party year in and year out, from habit and prejudice. Even if a man supports a party for its general principles, he must be independent enough to vote against a bad candidate that it nominates or a bad law that it advocates. This independent spirit has grown steadily. As you will see, our ballots are now arranged so as to recognize and assist it.

3. The Primary and Nominations

Platform and Primary – A party does two important things before every election. It makes a party platform, stating the principles for which its stands. It nominates, that is, names candidates through an election of its own called a primary. These candidates of a party are called its "ticket." Now think how this affects the election which follows. When you are eighteen and go to cast your first ballot, you can vote for anybody you please (as will be explained). But since the great mass of voters will vote for the party candidates, no one else stands a real chance of election and you will simply throw away your vote if you cast it for an outsider. So, really, the election has been narrowed down, long before it is held, to a choice between the party candidates who stand on the party platform.

Importance of the Primary – You see, therefore, how important is the primary. Altogether, too many Americans pay scant attention to the primaries, and then groan because they have such a poor choice on Election Day. The time to make the first choice is at this first election day, called the primary, which takes place months before the general election.

How Candidates are Chosen – The machinery of nominating candidates is very elaborate and has been much criticized. Under the older system, the members of the party elected delegates at the primary, then sent these delegates to nominating conventions. These conventions named the candidates. In recent years, "direct primaries" have been introduced where the members of the party name their candidates directly at the primary.

The National Conventions – The presidential candidates are nominated at a great national convention in which delegates from all the States sit. It takes place every four years in the summer preceding the election, and is one of our most stirring political events. The national platform is drawn up, and after much excitement, many speeches, and often prolonged balloting, the candidate is named. (The candidate for Vice-President is also named but, unfortunately, with little interest or attention from the delegates.) In most States the principle of the "direct primary" has been applied to presidential candidates, where the voters at the primary are not only electing their delegates to the national convention, but instructing them for whom to vote.

4. The Campaign

The Campaign – A presidential campaign creates great excitement. Meetings are held all over the country, and the candidates address great gatherings. Every voter has ample time to read and hear all the arguments, discuss them with his family and friends, and decide how he will vote on Election Day. The parties have national and State committees, which collect large sums to finance the campaigns and direct them.

Money has become the fuel that keeps the political machine running. Since modern campaigns have become so expensive due to their dependence on television, fund raising has become a major task of each candidate. Also, legal restrictions on wealthy givers has diminished, and the rapid rise of special-interest, and political action committees have made them indispensible to the quest for office.

In the 1970's, Congress passed stricter laws to govern campaign financing, and the Federal Election Commission was established to prevent the corrupt use of these large sums of money. Detailed records of all campaign income and expenditures are carefully checked by the commission. Money given by individuals has been limited to $1,000 each for the primary and general election campaigns of the candidates, and cash contributions over $100 may not be accepted.

Political action committees (PACs) were created because of a law which forbids corporations, labor unions and other special-interest groups to make direct campaign contributions. But these groups can give to PACs which, in turn, can contribute $5,000 (or $10,000 if there is a primary election) directly to the candidate which supports their political views. These committees are also free to spend as much money as they want, to support candidates, independent of the particular candidate's campaigns.

Congress has also established the Presidential Campaign Fund which was first used in the 1976 election, and comes from donations made by taxpayers each year as they fill out their federal income tax forms. The law requires each candidate to raise at least $5,000 (in contributions of $250 or less) in 20 States or more, to qualify for this public financing. The major political parties also receive federal funds to stage their national conventions. Even a minority party that gains 5% of the vote in a presidential campaign qualifies for these funds.

5. Registration and Election

Registration – There is one more preliminary to voting, and that is registration. In all but a few States, no citizen can vote unless he has previously entered his name on the voting list of his election district with his address, age, and other details. This is to prevent fraud. Vicious political bosses used to win elections by hiring criminals to vote in several election districts. These were called "repeaters." This trick is impossible when there is a registration list, for then either party can investigate and arrest any one guilty of fraudulent registration or, at any rate, prevent his voting on Election Day.

There are usually several registration days. It is obviously just as much the duty of every voter to register as to vote; for unless he does the former, he cannot do the latter.

In most jurisdictions, the registration list is usually carried over from one year to another, and it is not necessary to register unless you have moved into a new district.

Bribery – Repeating is but one form of fraud at elections. There is always a criminal class in every community willing to sell its votes. This is called bribery. The political boss who bribes and the man who takes the bribe are equally guilty of one of the gravest crimes. If convicted, they are heavily sentenced. Buying or selling a vote is one of the most dishonorable of all crimes – an act of treachery to one's country. Our land of fair play is entitled to every voter's honest judgment, but the sale of a vote is the destruction of a person's freedom and dignity.

The Secret Ballot – It is useless for a boss to give a bribe unless he can be sure that the vote paid for is delivered. Obviously, a person debased enough to be bribed, cannot be relied upon to vote as he promises. So long as voting was public, the briber could be sure of his vote. Public voting also made possible the control of the weak by the powerful. A man might lack the courage to vote as he thought he should, through fear of losing his job. Therefore, the secret ballot was invented. Originating in Australia, it spread throughout the United States in the 1890's, and most free nations. It is an ingenious system by which a person's vote is entirely his own secret. It leaves no way for anyone else to know how the individual has voted. Even if a person should wish to convince a boss that he has voted "right," he cannot do so under the secret ballot system. This secret ballot system was originally used with the paper ballot but, today, has been adapted for use with voting machines.

Main Features – There are three main features of the secret ballot:
1. All ballots of all parties are printed at public expense and given out to the voters, one by one, at the polls.
2. The voter marks his ballot, thus indicating his vote, alone in a booth or small compartment.
3. The ballot is then kept secret and deposited, so that no one can see how it is marked.

How It Works – Let us suppose that you are eighteen, that you have registered, that you have voted at your primary, and after having read, listened, and discussed, you have made up your mind about which candidates you wish to vote for in the main election. On Election Day, you go to the polling-place in your election district. The election officials (representing both parties) sit at a table with the list of registered voters before them. You give your name; it is checked off the list; you enter a booth; and you examine the official ballot. On it are the names of all the candidates. You vote by marking the ballot, punching the computer card by the names of the candidates you are supporting, or pulling the appropriate levers for the candidates of your choice (depending on the type of voting system used in your community). You can vote for someone not on the printed list by writing his name in a blank space provided for that purpose. Candidates that you choose by this process are known as "write-in" candidates. Having checked over your ballot to make sure you have voted as you wished, you fold over the ballot or place the computer punch card in its sleeve, leave the booth, and see it dropped in the ballot-box.

As an added precaution, a ballot is treated as void if marked other than as stated. The cross mark must be wholly within the allotted space, for instance. Thus, people who are bribed would forfeit their vote if they put some special mark on their ballots in an effort to prove to their boss that they voted as agreed.

At the end of the day – the polls are usually open from about sunrise to sunset – officials open the ballot-box and count the votes.

To prevent the "stuffing" of ballot-boxes with fraudulent votes, ballots are now usually numbered serially on detachable stubs. This stub is torn off as the ballot is cast and dropped in a separate box. The number of ballots and the number of stubs must always be equal, and a check on the number of ballots is routinely performed.

In addition to the election officials who give out the ballots, count them, and so on, each party having candidates on the ballots is allowed a certain number of "watchers" who have the right to watch the voting, to "challenge" the right of anyone to vote whom they have reason to suspect, and to watch the counting of the ballots.

If you are unable to vote on Election Day because you are out of town or have some type of illness or disability, you can still vote with an absentee ballot. This ballot can be obtained from county or city election officials. You indicate on the absentee ballot who you support and then, it must be returned to the election officials before election day. These ballots will then be counted with the rest of the ballots on election day.

Majority and Plurality – These words are often used carelessly as if they meant the same thing. "Majority" means more than half of all votes cast. "Plurality" means only more than any other candidate. If only two candidates are voted for, you can see that the person who has a plurality must also have the majority. But if more than two are running for office, let us say candidates A, B, and C, and A receives 4,000 votes, B 3,000, and C 2,000, no candidate has a majority (which would be 4,501 votes), but A has a plurality of 1,000 votes over B. The general rule in America is that only a plurality is needed to be elected. In this case, therefore, A would be declared the winner.

However, some States and municipalities require candidates to gain a majority of the votes to win certain types of elections. If no candidate were to win a majority of the votes, a run-off election between the top two candidates would be necessary to determine the winner. Using the above example, A and B would be required to participate in a run-off election to determine who is the winner.

The New York and Massachusetts Ballots – There are many kinds of ballots in the various States. The two principal kinds are the New York ballots which were introduced in 1910 and 1918, when a reform took place in that State. In the first ballot, you will see that the candidates are arranged by tickets, and the voter who wishes to vote a straight ticket has only to put one cross in the circle above his party column. This system favors the straight-ticket, or single party vote. The second ballot, which originated in the State of Massachusetts, is the kind where the names are arranged by offices, not by tickets. A voter must make a choice for each candidate. This favors independent voting, for every voter has to look over the whole ballot, whether he wishes to or not.

Note that both New York ballots use party symbols to indicate the party candidates. In Massachusetts, the ballots used have no such symbols. (Each State has its own peculiarities in the form of its ballots.)

Who Can Vote – As we saw under State powers and laws, each State has the right to say who shall vote, barring the one exception of the Fifteenth Amendment, designed to insure the right to vote for all citizens regardless "of race, color, or previous condition of servitude." In the early days of the republic, there were many restrictions. Only men with property were allowed to vote. Gradually, as America began to grow, the demand for the vote came from all classes. By 1850, all white males were able to vote, but most States did not allow blacks to vote. In 1868, all blacks were granted citizenship, enabling all men to vote in every State. For many years, voting was restricted only to men, but the Nineteenth Amendment was added to the national Constitution in 1920 giving women the right to vote throughout the country. In 1964, the poll tax was abolished as a requirement for voting in national elections. The right to vote was also extended to all citizens of eighteen years of age or older in 1971. A number of other States used to have certain literacy requirements as well. For example, Massachusetts used to require a voter to be able to read a section of the State constitution and write his own name. However, all literacy tests have been done away with. Today, the requirements are few:

1.   **Citizenship** – Only Americans, by birth or naturalization, can vote.
2.   **Age** – Voters must be eighteen years old.
3.   **Residence** – It is required that a person live within a State a certain period of time, generally for thirty days, before voting. There are further restrictions within each State, by which a voter must have resided in a particular State, and an election district, a certain length of time.

Certain classes of people are kept from voting, such as insane or retarded people and criminals who have been convicted of a felony (that is, a serious crime). Aliens, of course, cannot vote, no matter how long they remain in the country, since they are not American citizens. A few States used to make a small exception, allowing aliens who have taken out their first papers to vote.

Citizenship and Naturalization – It must be understood that citizenship does not depend on voting. Boys and girls whose parents are Americans or who were born in this country of whatever parentage are just as much American citizens as any voter. So are other Americans, whether permitted to vote or not. They are members of our nation; that is what citizenship means. As we learned in discussing the difference between civil and political rights, they are entitled to every protection and privilege.

Every foreigner who intends to stay in the United States should become a citizen, as soon as possible. Until the person does so, he or she is not entitled to the full rights of an American. This is just as important to the individual's success, safety, and happiness as the need to learn to read and write English.

The citizen-to-be must first file an application for naturalization. This statement declares that the individual is over 18 years old, is ready to give up his or her former citizenship, and intends to become a United States citizen. After five years of residing in this country, the citizen-to-be files a second statement including personal data and two testimonies from U.S. citizens stating the applicant's good character. At this time, the person signs statements renouncing former citizenship and swearing that he or she has never belonged to a group bent on the violent overthrow of the U.S. government. Finally, the applicant appears before the federal judge, after passing a test which shows knowledge of the English language and the American system of government. The individual recites the oath of allegiance to the United States of America, and the judge awards a certificate of citizenship to each new American. All naturalized citizens have the same rights and privileges as natural born citizens, except that they cannot become President of the United States.

Children under 16 years of age become citizens automatically when their parents are naturalized. But if they were born in America, they are citizens anyway. A wife becomes a citizen when her husband is naturalized. A woman can become naturalized by the same process as a man. Note that foreign-born spouses of American citizens need to reside only three years before applying.

Election Dates – The presidential election comes every four years on the Tuesday, after the first Monday, in November. The State, county, and township elections usually come in off years, in November. So do most city elections. New England town elections and most village elections come in the spring. As the length of the terms of governor and other offices varies greatly with the different States, no general rule can be laid down. But it is the tendency, nowadays, to have a local election when there is no presidential election; for local elections are questions of personal uprightness and business ability rather than of national issues, which are controlled by party politics. Therefore, it is wiser to hold local elections at a time when party politics is not uppermost in every voter's mind.

In local elections communities often forget party lines altogether and nominate a joint non-partisan ticket.

The school elections often come at a separate time, usually at the annual meeting of the parents and tax payers. Politics should not, and usually does not, have any place in these elections.

Some voters are too careless or indifferent to vote for lesser officers. This is not to do one's full duty, however. A good American should follow the elections closely, and vote at every one. As we have seen, the local elections and the State elections often affect the voter's welfare even more closely than do the national elections.

6. Direct Government

Our Representative Government – All the elections, thus far described, are to choose people to occupy the various offices of our government. These people represent us for the term of their office and make our laws, execute them, and interpret them for us and in our name. Under this system, the people make the laws; but they do it indirectly through these representatives. That is why our government is a republic and not a "pure democracy" like the New England town meeting.

Direct Lawmaking – There has been a movement in a number of States in recent years to enable the people to make laws directly, when they so desire. Obviously, all the voters of a State cannot gather in a meeting and discuss and vote. The processes used are called the "initiative" and the "referendum." By the initiative, a group of voters can draft a law; and on securing the signatures of a certain required number of voters, the group can have the law submitted to the voters at the next election. The law is printed on the ballot and the voters vote "Yes" or "No" on it. If a majority vote "Yes," it becomes law. In this operation, the legislature has no voice whatever. A number of cities apply the initiative to city ordinances.

By the referendum, a group of voters who do not approve of a law passed by the legislature can force its submission to a sort of popular veto. They prepare a petition for a referendum, and on securing the signatures of a certain required number of voters, the law must be referred to the people at the next election. This petition is also required for amendments and public opinion surveys. The referendum is printed on the ballot, as in the case of the initiative, and becomes a law only when there are more votes for, than against it.

The referendum is new as applied to laws, but it is a very old system of amending our State constitutions. After the amendments have been proposed, they are printed on the ballot and voted upon exactly as above. In recent years, the referendum procedure has also been used occasionally to ask the public's opinion on various questions by a vote that is non-binding.

The Recall – This is an additional device for giving the people more direct control over their elective officers. If a group does not approve of the course of a mayor or governor, for instance, and can obtain a required number of signatures of voters to a petition, the mayor or governor must submit to a new election forthwith, and he loses the office if a majority then vote against him. The decisions of judges on constitutional points, etc., have also been submitted to the recall. The recall has not made as much headway as the initiative and referendum.

Not a "Pure Democracy" – Even with all these new devices, our government continues to be essentially representative in character. These processes are only supplemental to the work of the legislature, governors, and other officers. The advisability of these "direct" methods is one of the most frequent questions of the day.

Questions on the Text

Section 1

1.　What is the basis of our government?
2.　What are the two reasons why every American should vote?

Section 2

3.　What causes parties to grow?
4.　Do all Americans belong to parties?
5.　What are the two main parties today?

6.   What were the two main parties in the first years of the republic?
7.   Are they related in any way?
8.   What has been the lasting issue between these parties?
9.   When did the present Republican party originate and for what cause?
10.   What other parties can you name?
11.   Why should a voter be independent?

Section 3

12.   What is a platform?
13.   What is done at a primary?
14.   How does a primary limit the voter's choice on election day?
15.   What is a "direct" primary?
16.   What is the other system of making nominations?
17.   How are the presidential candidates named?

Section 4

18.   Describe a presidential campaign.
19.   What restrictions are there on contributions to candidates?
20.   What is the object of these restrictions?

Section 5

21.   What is registration?
22.   What is its object?
23.   What is a repeater?
24.   Why is it important for a voter to register?
25.   What is bribery and why is it a most dishonorable crime?
26.   Are the briber and the person who is bribed equally guilty?
27.   What is the purpose of Secret Ballot?
28.   What are the three main features by which it obtains secrecy?
29.   Describe the operation of voting.
30.   Must you vote for the candidates of the parties or is it possible to vote for some one else?
31.   What is the difference between a majority and a plurality?
32.   What is a voting-machine?
33.   Describe the Massachusetts ballot.
34.   What other kind is used?
35.   Which ballot fosters independent voting and why?
36.   What restrictions on voting were there in the early days of the nation and by what year were they removed?
37.   What are the three requirements for voting?
38.   Can aliens vote in any States?
39.   How many States give women the right to vote?
40.   Are illiterates generally allowed to vote or not?
41.   What is a citizen?

42. How can a foreigner become an American citizen?
43. Are children born in America of foreign parents American citizens or not?
44. What classes are disenfranchised altogether?
45. When is the main election day?
46. When are State, county, township, and city elections usually held?
47. When are village and town elections usually held?
48. When are school elections usually held?
49. Why should a voter vote at all elections?

Section 6

50. What is the initiative?
51. What is the referendum?
52. How has the referendum been used for amending our State constitutions?
53. What is the recall?
54. Has the introduction of these direct methods given us a "pure democracy"?

Questions for Discussion

1. What qualifications does the Bible give for candidates seeking election?
2. Do you know which parties the members of your family belong to?
3. How much should a son's vote be influenced by his father's?
4. Can you name any other parties than those in the text?
5. What parties are there in your State?
6. Which party won the last presidential election?
7. Which won the last State election?
8. Which won the last local election?
9. Has there ever been a non-partisan ticket in your community?
10. Examine a national party platform and see what it contains?
11. Why is there often prolonged balloting in a national convention?
12. Can you name the presidential candidates in the last election?
13. Did you ever attend a big political meeting?
14. Do you know where the polls are in your election district?
15. Do you think illiterates should vote?

Test 7

96

CHAPTER 17

Taxation

Government Must Take Before It Can Give

Government, through taxation and borrowing (which is delayed taxation), takes from individuals: (1) the goods and services required by government workers, pensioners, and public charges, and (2) the tools needed for such projects as the vast interstate highway network, or the Tennessee Valley authority which provides cheap electricity, flood control, and irrigation for the entire Tennessee River basin.

In exchange for taxes, the government gives the people the services of government workers and the use of such things as roads, parks, etc.

These forced exchanges between government and the individual are unavoidable in modern society, because citizens give authority to the government to take from one group and give to another.

When people grant this power to the government, one of their most difficult problems is to prevent government from becoming a heavy burden on the productive worker. It is all the more difficult, because the taxation is frequently caused by political pressure groups demanding gifts from the public purse.

This demand forces government into a hard choice: If it does not increase governmental taking, it cannot increase governmental giving as demanded by the pressure groups; if it does increase governmental taking, it is only a matter of time until the people, including the individuals within the pressure groups, rise up in violent protest against such excessive taxation.

The inconsistency of the people in demanding that the government give without taking has always been a great pitfall for self-government.

Government, in order to be a government, must have a monopoly on the legal use of force, and by its very nature must make this force the basis of all its dealings with the private citizen. Therefore, as George Washington rightly proclaimed, "Like fire, [government] is a dangerous servant and a fearful master."

The history of liberty is a history of limitations of governmental power, not the increase of it. Therefore, when citizens resist the concentration of power, they are helping to preserve liberty. There is not a single instance in the history of mankind in which a body of sinful men, endowed with unchecked power, chose to use that power to preserve the God-govern liberties of the people.

1. The Taxpayer

Every One Pays Taxes – Many people think that they do not pay taxes, because they own no property and never pay anything directly to a tax collector. If they vote for some wasteful city improvement, they think that they will pay nothing toward the expense of it; and the cost will fall upon others. However, they fool themselves because everyone pays a tax. In fact, every boy and girl has paid a tax without knowing it.

This is because most taxes are shifted; that is, the man who pays the tax collects it afterward from someone else. Take the best known of all taxes, the tax on real estate, land, and houses. The owner of the land and house pays the tax, and you might think that if you rent a house or an apartment, you pay no tax at all. To the contrary, many landlords add part or all of the tax for the house into the rent; and the tenant, without realizing it, pays the real estate tax. (The tax on the land itself cannot usually be shifted and is, therefore, called a "direct" tax. Taxes which can be shifted are called "indirect" taxes.)

More subtle and concealed is the tariff. As we have seen, this is both a protection to American industries and a tax. The importer of the foreign made goods pays the tax to the national government; and then, collects it from the retailer, who collects it from you. The tariff, you see, is part of his cost, just as much as is the price paid the foreign manufacturer. If you ever bought a doll or any toy made in Germany you paid such a tax. Every time you buy imported chocolate, you pay a tax – a small item; but since the chocolate came from abroad, a tariff was paid up on entering the country. So it is for any number of common products imported from other countries, such as silk, woolen goods, sugar, tin, fur, rubber, and so on.

2. The National Taxes

What Is Taxed – The national government collects its own taxes and the States collect theirs, as you might guess from what we have learned about our double system of government. The national taxes have normally been of three kinds:

1. Customs duties on imports (that is, the tariff).
2. Excise taxes on whiskey and tobacco. (An excise tax is a tax on a domestic product—an internal revenue tax, as it is called in our laws.)
3. Taxes on incomes of corporations and individuals.

In war time, when the expenses of the national government are very high, taxes are levied on many other things—automobiles, motion pictures, theater tickets, jewelry, and other luxuries. An inheritance tax has also been used by the national government, that is, a tax on all the property of a person who dies. However, this type of tax is very unpopular and is seldom used by modern politicians.

The national government's power of taxation is granted in the broadest terms (Art. I, Sec. 8, Par. 1), which includes the power to tax real estate throughout the country. The federal government has done so at times, but now leaves this up to the States for their chief source of revenue.

One of the few restrictions is stated in the Constitution, which requires that customs duties and excise taxes shall be uniform throughout the country (Art. I, Sec. 8, Par. 1). Another requirement is that "direct" taxes be apportioned among the States according to population (Art.I, Sec. 9, Par. 4). This has an historic importance because it delayed the imposition of a national income tax for many years. The Supreme Court decided in 1895, after much argument, that an income tax was a "direct" tax and since Congress had not apportioned the tax according to population, the law was declared unconstitutional. (Income being unequally distributed among the States, such tax apportioned according to population would not be fair). The Sixteenth Amendment to the Constitution, passed in 1913, removed this restriction upon income taxes and an income tax has now become a large source of national revenue. Congress is also prohibited from taxing exports (Art. I, Sec. 9, Par. 5).

Customs Duties – These are fixed in a lengthy schedule contained in a bill passed by Congress. The rates vary widely. Many articles enter duty free. The duties are collected at the custom-houses in our ports upon the arrival of the goods. These duties have long been the principal source of the national revenue.

Bonds – The revenue from taxes should be sufficient to cover all that is needed to run the government in ordinary times. A war, however, involves such large resources that it must be financed, in part, by borrowing money. This is done through the issue of government bonds, which are simply the government's promise to pay a certain sum with interest after a certain number of years. The Liberty Loans of World War I were made by the people loaning money to the government, and receiving in return, Liberty Bonds. The total of bonds owed by a government is called its "national debt." All the great countries of the world had large national debts after World War I and II. At the present time, due to the reckless spending of our national government, our national debt is over four trillion dollars!

For the construction of large permanent structures which will last for generations, like the Panama Canal, bonds are rightly issued. To pay for such an improvement, in a few years, would greatly increase the tax rate. A bond issue spreads this tax burden over many years.

3. State and Local Taxes

Prior to the twentieth century, the real estate or land tax was commonly regarded by many Americans as immoral, because it violates the teaching of Scripture which declares that "the earth is the Lord's." Property taxes were considered to be Anti-family, Anti-God, and Anti-private property. Many Americans fail to realize that the power to tax a piece of property dictates who is ultimately in control of the property. The power to tax property is the power to confiscate property. (Modern American homeowners are now beginning to force their county governments to limit their annual increase in the real estate tax, because they are unable to afford to live in their homes!)

Real Estate – Because many twentieth century Americans are ignorant of, or indifferent to, the Bible's teaching on land taxes, the major source of local revenue has now become a tax on real estate. The collection of this is usually turned over to the local authorities, town, or county. Therefore, a real estate tax, assessed and paid locally, often includes four different taxes; village, school, town or township, and county. Property taxes may also be assessed for local independent agencies (i.e., library boards) and on rare occasions, the State. The officers of each of the divisions fix the amount of tax required to meet the needs of their division.

Tax Rate – The first item to be settled, before a tax rate is fixed, is the value of the property covered by it. Assessors do this, lot by lot, house by house. Their record is called a "tax roll" or "list." Opportunity is always given for protest by the owner against the size of his assessment. Certain property, such as schools, libraries, hospitals, and churches, is usually tax exempt. Let us say that the total assessed value of all the real estate in a town is fixed at $3,000,000. Now the amounts needed are as follows:

Schools	$22,000
Town (roads, salaries, etc.)	20,000
County (roads, salaries, etc.)	10,000
State (highways, salaries, etc.)	8,000
Total	$60,000

If $3,000,000 of property must yield $60,000 in taxes, each dollar must obviously pay 2 cents. The tax rate is, therefore, 2 percent, or as it is commonly written, $2.00–tax expressed in dollars and cents per every one hundred dollars.

If your house and lot are assessed at $50,000, your share of the tax will be $1,000.

Collection – The tax is paid to the tax-collector, who turns over the amounts to the town treasurer, who retains the town's share and pays over what is due to the treasurers of the county and the State. The collector has a right to sell property in order to collect taxes. Although this right is somewhat limited, many older Americans on fixed incomes have been forced to leave their own homes or farms as their property was confiscated. This is only one of many reasons why land taxes are anti-family.

Personal Property Tax – This used to be very generally collected on every sort of property, household furniture, stocks, bonds, and so on. It is still carried on the books of most tax districts, but in practice is collected only from wealthy householders and large owners of stocks and bonds. It is an unsatisfactory tax, for it is very difficult to assess fairly (since personal property is easily concealed), and it has fallen into disuse.

Income Tax vs. Head Tax – Most States impose taxes on personal incomes, thus subjecting citizens to a double tax since the national government also taxes incomes. A better form of a personal tax is known as a head tax. This tax has an annual flat rate that is assessed to all citizens who are eligible to vote, regardless of their specific income. This type of personal head tax has historically helped to keep government from raising taxes on its citizens too quickly, for the government is forced to keep taxes low enough so that even low-income families can afford them. This form of taxation also provides a natural incentive for low-income families to work hard and earn extra income. Sadly, few States utilize this simplified form of taxation at the present time.

Sales Tax – Many States are also beginning to increase the use of county wide sales taxes to generate revenue. This tax is paid directly by individual consumers at the point that they purchase merchandise of any kind. It is the responsibility of business owners to collect and pay the tax to the State at specified times during the year. The sales tax is based on a fixed rate of roughly 3 to 8 percent, depending on the particular States' tax rate.

Corporation Tax – Many States tax the corporations doing business within them. It is levied in various ways, sometimes on the capital stock, sometimes on the income. In this latter form, it duplicates the national tax on corporation incomes.

Licenses and Fees. – These are small taxes collected by a government usually in connection with some act performed by the government. The fee for a dog license pays for the pound keeper and eliminates stray dogs. A marriage license covers the expense of keeping marriage records. High license fees for saloons used to bring in large revenues for some States, with the hope to reduce their number. Fees must also be paid for having a deed or other documents recorded in the county records.

Franchise Taxes – A franchise is a privilege given to a person or corporation to use public property, for instance, to a cable television company to build satellite transmitters and run electronic lines on a public street. Some cities tax such franchises heavily. Chicago, for example, receives more than $1,000,000 a year by taxing the earnings of cable television companies.

Assessment. – The cost of local improvements for sewers, new streets, etc., is usually assessed against the nearby property owners in proportion to the special benefit, which they will receive as a result. These payments are called "special assessments." They are not like other taxes, because they are not equally applied to all property owners but are collected from the few especially benefited.

Bonds – All our local governments issue bonds to pay for permanent improvements. The purpose is exactly the same as in the case of national bond issues. If a new school is built costing $2,000,000, it is not right that taxes should increase substantially to pay such a large sum in a year or two of its construction. Therefore the school district issues bonds to borrow the money. The same is true of sewers, water works, and all lasting improvements. Our great cities have huge outstanding debts as a result.

It is so simple to issue bonds that communities are often tempted to pay for temporary improvements in this fashion. This is unsound and puts a heavy burden on later generations because interest has to be paid regularly. The principal of every bond must be paid off when due. For this purpose, "sinking funds" must be established;

which means that everybody must be taxed, not only to pay the current interest, but also, to put aside an additional sum each year to the principal when the bond falls due. Issuing bonds is mortgaging future generations, and a community should be very careful that future taxpayers will share the benefit.

Eminent Domain – Suppose a new railroad or street is needed. It must run across the private property of a number of home owners. Suppose these owners do not wish to sell–even though the public will clearly benefit. Can the nation, State or town, take this private property for this public purpose? It can, and this power is called the right of "eminent domain." The only limitations are that the public need shall be established by an impartial body, and that the owner shall be paid the value of his land. The legal proceedings by which these facts are determined are called "condemnation proceedings." The owner is protected from the arbitrary taking of his property without proper compensation by the Fifth Amendment to the national Constitution (Art. V, final clause).

Questions on the Text

Section 1

1. How many people pay taxes?
2. What is the difference between a direct tax and an indirect tax and how is a tax shifted?
3. Can you illustrate how a tax is shifted in the case of a tax on a house and in the case of the tariff?

Section 2

4. What are the three principal taxes of the national government?
5. What other taxes have been used in war time?
6. What constitutional restriction is there on the levying of customs duties and excise taxes?
7. What constitutional restriction is there on levying of direct taxes?
8. How did this delay the income tax?
9. Can Congress tax exports?
10. What has been the principal source of national revenue?
11. Where are customs duties collected?
12. Upon what articles have excise taxes been laid by the national government, and who collects them?
13. Upon whom does the national government levy an income tax?
14. Why does the government issue bonds and when is it justifiable?
15. What is the national debt?
16. How was the Panama Canal paid for?
17. Why was this method justifiable?

Section 3

18. What is the chief source of State revenue?
19. What government levies and collects this tax?

20. What divisions share in this tax?
21. How is a tax-roll made, who makes it, and what is it?
22. What property is exempt from taxation?
23. Given the total assessed valuation of a town, how is the tax rate figured?
24. What is done with the tax when collected?
25. How can a tax-collector enforce payment of tax?
26. Why is a land tax immoral and anti-family?
27. Give some illustrations of licenses and fees.
28. What is a franchise tax?
29. What is an assessment and how does it differ from a tax?
30. For what purposes should local governments issue bonds?
31. Why is it unfair to future taxpayers to pay for temporary improvements with bonds?
32. What is the right of eminent domain?
33. What are the two limitations on it?
34. What law enforces these limitations?

ILLINOIS TAX REVENUES FOR 1993

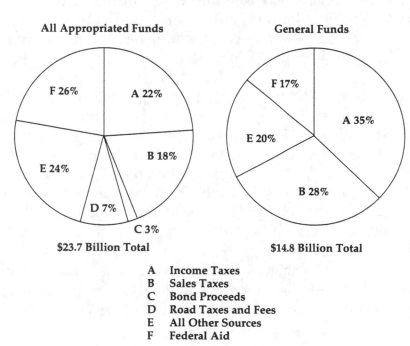

All Appropriated Funds

General Funds

F 26%   A 22%
E 24%   B 18%
D 7%   C 3%

$23.7 Billion Total

F 17%   A 35%
E 20%   B 28%

$14.8 Billion Total

A Income Taxes
B Sales Taxes
C Bond Proceeds
D Road Taxes and Fees
E All Other Sources
F Federal Aid

REVENUES

The State of Illinois will most likely collect $23.7 billion in total revenue from state and federal sources in Fiscal Year 1993. General fund receipts are expected to total $14.8 billion.

Income and sales taxes are the two major sources of state revenues, representing approximately 40 percent of the total receipts.

The next largest source of state revenues is federal aid in the form of reimbursements for federally-supported expenditures or in direct support of particular programs. More than 50 percent of the federal reimbursements is for welfare expenditures, including the assessments program implemented in Fiscal Year 1992.

Other major revenue sources include public utility taxes, cigarette taxes, lottery receipts, insurance taxes and fees, university tuition and fees, and interest on investments. Also included is $300 million in short-term borrowing proceeds.

Motor vehicle registration and drivers license fees together with motor fuel taxes are the primary components of the road taxes and fees category.

Test 8

CHAPTER 18

Courts and Trials

1. The Two Kinds of Laws

Civil Laws – If a gang of rowdy teenagers, old enough to know better, set fire to a barn for the fun of seeing a blaze, they break two different kinds of laws and commit two different kinds of wrongs. They damage the owner of the barn, for they destroy it and he is that much poorer. He, therefore, has the right to sue them for damages in what is called a "civil" suit. (To sue is simply to seek justice in a court, and a suit is the process of doing this.) This law – that we must not destroy another's property and that if we do, he can go to court and compel us to pay for the damage done – is called a "civil" law. You see that this wrong is done to an individual.

Criminal Laws – But a wrong has also been done to the people of the State in which the barn is located. The whole community is imperilled and injured by having such hoodlums about. Nobody's barn is safe. Therefore, the law of the State says that the act of setting fire to a barn is a crime to be punished by imprisonment. The gang members have, therefore, broken a "criminal" law, as well as, a "civil" law.

Points of Difference – This distinction is important and runs throughout the law. In a civil suit, the plaintiff (who sues) and the defendant (who is sued) are both individuals. In a criminal suit the people, styled "The People of the State of New York," for instance, are the plaintiff, and the accused person is the defendant. If the crime is against the nation, counterfeiting, for instance, "The People of the United States" are the plaintiff. In a civil suit, each side hires his own lawyer and pays his own expenses. In a criminal suit, the "People of the State" are represented by the District Attorney, a public officer elected by the county. The defendant hires his own counsel. In a civil suit, the object is to recover damages, or in some cases, prevent damage. In a criminal suit, the object is to convict the defendant of a crime and have him fined or imprisoned. (A fine is a money payment to the State. It is imposed as a punishment and to prevent a repetition of the act, and not to recompense anybody.)

2. A Criminal Trial

The Crime – Let us suppose that a murder has been committed in your village. A respected storekeeper going home on Saturday night with his cash from the safe has been struck on the head, killed, and robbed. His body is found at midnight by a policeman. The murderer has vanished. Let us now see what legal steps follow, remembering that all these matters are left to the individual States to decide, and that the details vary with every State.

The Coroner's Inquest – The first public inquiry is made by the coroner, an officer of the county whose business it is to inquire into every mysterious death. He summons six or twelve men to act as a coroner's jury and holds what is called a

"Coroner's Inquest." Witnesses are called, and the jury reports what they think has been the cause of death–"from a blow struck by a person unknown," for instance. This is usually a brief and unimportant process.

The Arrest – Meantime, the district attorney of the county and the county detectives, as well as, the local police have been hard at work. Within a few days a man brings suspicion on himself through the lavish spending of money, and it is found that he lives not far from the scene of the crime. The police can arrest him at once on reasonable suspicion, and they do arrest him if there is any fear that the suspect will escape. (Can a private citizen make an arrest? Only if a crime is actually committed in his presence.) Here the district attorney goes privately to a judge and secures a warrant (that is an order) for the man's arrest. The police arrest the man and lock him up.

If this happens in a large city, the prisoner is at once photographed, fingerprinted, and a computerized background check is done to see if he has ever committed a crime before.

A Prisoner's Rights – Here in jail, the law at once begins to protect the prisoner from injustice. It provides that a prisoner, when questioned, must be warned that everything he says may be used against him; and that if this warning is not given or if force or duress (that is, threats or torture amounting to force) is used, nothing that the prisoner says can be used against him.

As soon as he is arrested, a prisoner is entitled to the advice of counsel. Many other safeguards will appear later. They are all based on the broad idea that every man is to be presumed innocent until he is proven guilty. That is something we should all remember and apply, for it holds true in every day life just as much as in a trial in court. It is one of the noblest principles of the splendid body of Biblically-based law, which we have inherited from England. It is almost impossible that any honest, well-meaning American will ever be falsely accused and arrested. But if he is, his very life may depend upon our wise and benign system of law which protects the innocent just as zealously as it seeks out the guilty.

Habeas Corpus – These Latin words mean "Have the body." It is a writ, that is an order, issued by a judge requiring the officers of a jail to bring a prisoner before him. "Have the body brought before the court" is the full idea. The purpose is to prevent unlawful arrest and imprisonment. If a prisoner does not know why he was arrested or whether he is legally detained, he can find out by obtaining this writ. The court must investigate and decide whether the prisoner is legally held. If illegally held, he must set him free. This is an old English writ of the greatest importance to our liberties.

The national Constitution protects it in Article I, Section 9, Paragraph 2. Yet, there is also a clear recognition that, in time of war, private rights must give way to public safety. Under these conditions, Congress can suspend the right to the writ and permit imprisonment without the necessity of explaining why.

Arraignment – The prisoner is next brought into court before a justice of the peace (in a city before a police magistrate), and a brief hearing is given to the evidence. If the crime charged were a minor one (disorderly conduct or a violation of a speed law), the justice of the peace could go ahead and try the case and find the defendant guilty or not guilty. But the charge being a serious crime, he can only decide whether the prisoner shall or shall not be "held for the grand jury," that is, kept in jail until the grand jury can hear the evidence. If there is no evidence, he sets the prisoner free.

Bail – In the case of ordinary crimes, a prisoner can be released on bail while awaiting further action. That is, his friends who own property can sign a bond in an amount fixed by the court, agreeing to produce the defendant in court when he is wanted, or forfeit the sum named. (A defendant is said to "jump his bail" if he runs away.) Murder is such a serious charge that a prisoner accused of it is not admitted to bail.

The Grand Jury – This is the first part of our jury system. It is composed of not less than twelve or more than twenty-three citizens. The district attorney brings the State's witnesses before this body and presents the case to them. The grand jury sits in secret and hears only the side of the prosecution. The defendant's case is not heard. If at least twelve of the grand jury believe that the prisoner ought to be tried for the murder, the district attorney draws up an indictment making the charge of murder against the prisoner, and the foreman writes across the back of the indictment the words "A True Bill."

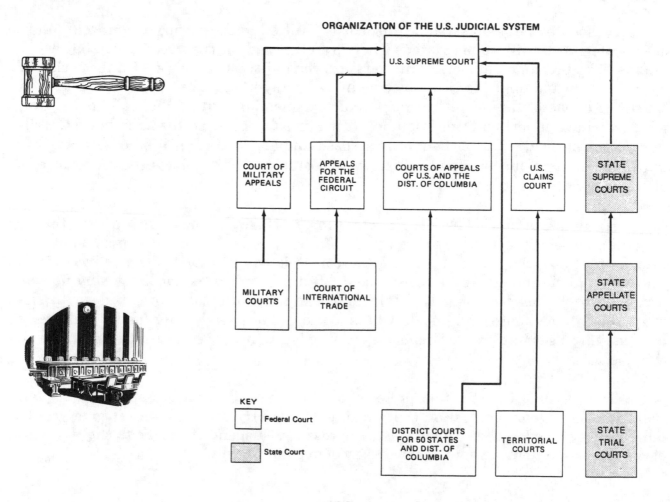

ORGANIZATION OF THE U.S. JUDICIAL SYSTEM

U.S. SUPREME COURT

COURT OF MILITARY APPEALS

APPEALS FOR THE FEDERAL CIRCUIT

COURTS OF APPEALS OF U.S. AND THE DIST. OF COLUMBIA

U.S. CLAIMS COURT

STATE SUPREME COURTS

MILITARY COURTS

COURT OF INTERNATIONAL TRADE

STATE APPELLATE COURTS

KEY

Federal Court

State Court

DISTRICT COURTS FOR 50 STATES AND DIST. OF COLUMBIA

TERRITORIAL COURTS

STATE TRIAL COURTS

This is not a trial of the defendant's guilt or innocence, you see. After indictment, as before, the defendant is still "presumed to be innocent." The grand jury has simply decided that enough evidence exists to require the prisoner's trial. It is another protection of the innocent; the theory being that no one man, not even a public official like the district attorney, should be able to make a citizen stand trial.

The Plea – The defendant is now brought before the court to "plead." The indictment is read to him, and he is asked whether he is "Guilty or not guilty." If he pleads "guilty" that is the end, and the court proceeds to sentence him without trial.

The Trial – If he pleads "Not guilty," the trial may not take place for months since the lawyers have much work to do preparing their cases. To compel witnesses to attend, a "subpoena," for each, is issued by the court commanding him to appear at the trial. This is "served upon" (i.e., handed to) the witness on behalf of the lawyer who wishes him to be present. A subpoena must always be obeyed. It is a serious offense to disregard any order of a court.

On the day fixed by the judge, the defendant is brought into court and the trial begins. The whole proceedings must be public, so they may be watched, and no Star-Chamber action may take place (Star Chamber was a royal tribunal that was abolished in 1641, notorious for secret sessions without jury). Also, the defendant must be present throughout. He sits with his counsel facing judge, witness, and jury.

The Trial Jury – This is the second and more important part of our jury system. It is sometimes called the "petit jury," which means "small jury" to distinguish it from the grand jury. It contains either six or twelve members.

The jury is chosen from "talesmen," that is, citizens summoned to court as possible jurymen. Their names are drawn by lot, thereby decreasing the chance of bribery or bias; and they are questioned one by one as called by the lawyers and the court. Friends of the defendant or the lawyers, or any one who might have difficulty in giving a fair decision, are ruled out by the court. Each side has also a limited number of "challenges"; that is, each side has the right to exclude a certain number of talesmen without any cause given, simply because the lawyer does not believe they would be favorable to his side. This jury weighs the evidence and decides the issues of trial, so that a fair decision might be made.

The Evidence – The district attorney opens the case with a speech in which he states what he proposes to prove. He then calls the State's witnesses one by one. Each witness is seated in the witness-chair, a high seat between the judge and the jury. A witness is said to "take the stand" when he enters the witness-chair. He is sworn "to tell the truth, the whole truth and nothing but the truth." If you are ever called as a witness, that must be your sole effort. Whether you have friends in the trial or are interested yourself makes no difference. Any one who tells anything but the truth commits perjury, the crime of false swearing; a very serious offense before God and men.

Now, a witness may give his evidence in court in only one way and according to a great many very technical rules, called the rules of evidence. For the first point, a witness is not allowed to volunteer anything. He must answer only the questions put to him. This often seems a slow and silly method to outsiders. But the reason is clear. Only by this method is it possible to keep the witness from blurting out prejudices, guesses, and remote facts that the jury ought not to pay any attention to. Only questions that call for proper evidence are allowed. Others are ruled out.

Experience has long shown that certain kinds of testimony can be believed and certain kinds cannot. The best illustration is hearsay, which the rules of evidence exclude (except in exceptional cases). Hearsay is second-hand evidence; that is, the witness tries to tell not what he, himself, saw or heard, but what somebody else saw and related to him. Gossip is typical hearsay and everybody knows how unreliable it is. A story always grows as it is handed on. So the law insists that no hearsay should be admitted, that the person who saw or heard must be produced in court. The basic objection to hearsay, you see, is that it is not sworn to; for the man who started the story is not in court.

There are many other rules of evidence which must be obeyed. The lawyers must follow them in their questions; and if a witness tries to evade them, his answers are stricken out of the court record.

Direct and Cross Examination. – The district attorney first puts on the stand the policeman who found the body, and asks questions that bring out what the policeman saw and did on that night. This is called the "direct examination." Counsel for the defendant then, has the right to cross-examine the policeman; that is, question him about what he has told and try to bring out facts more favorable to his client. Or if a witness is not telling the truth, he can often be tripped into a contradiction and thus, shown up as a liar.

Let us say that no witness of the crime can be produced. There is then no "direct" evidence. But the "circumstantial" evidence may be strong. That is, a weapon stained with blood, shown to have produced the wound that caused the death of the victim, and found on the defendant, is all circumstantial evidence. Also, a document that was in the victim's pocket is found on the defendant. Such evidence is often just as damning as direct evidence.

The Defense – After all the witnesses for the State have testified and been cross-examined, the prosecution rests. The defense opens with the speech by the defendant's lawyer and the defendant's witnesses are called, in turn, exactly as the State's were. The district attorney can cross-examine these witnesses, just as, the defendant's counsel could cross-examine the State's witnesses.

One of the most common defenses is an "alibi," that is, evidence that the defendant was somewhere else other than the place of the crime at the time it was committed. The defendant's neighbor takes the stand and swears that he saw him at his house around ten o'clock, the hour of the murder.

Can the defendant testify in his own behalf? He has the right, but he seldom does. Even an innocent man is apt to become confused with so much at stake and, therefore, the law provides that no defendant can be compelled to testify against himself in any criminal case. This is another protection that the law throws about the defendant. The Fifth Amendment in the Bill of Rights provides this protection.

The Summing Up – Both sides now sum up, the lawyer for the defense, first; the district attorney, last. These speeches are addressed to the jury and are often very eloquent pleas.

The Judge's Charge – Finally the judge "charges" the jury, that is, tells them what the law of the case is. Here is an interesting and important distinction. The judge lays down the law; the jury decides every question of fact. The judge is not even permitted to express an opinion on a question of fact. Let us give an illustration: The judge's charge might explain the different degrees of murder. These are carefully planned so as to inflict a punishment proportionate to the crime. Thus, for murder in the first degree (often punishable by death) there must be, not only an intent to kill, but premeditation (i.e., some planning and reflection). Killing in a sudden burst of anger without forethought is not considered as horrible a crime as killing in cold blood. This is considered murder in the second degree being punishable by life imprisonment, not death. The charge is part of the law which the judge must set forth and the jury should consider. However, each person on the jury has the power to sit in judgement of the facts and the law involved in each case. This total power of the jury gives the people an extra protection against bad or immoral laws that may have been passed by Congress, or handed down by a previous Supreme Court. No juror should ever feel forced to rule against a defendant based upon an immoral or unconstitutional law.

On the other hand, it is for the jury to decide whether the neighbor is telling the truth, or is possibly mistaken – whether the alibi is true or false. On this decision may depend the verdict and it is wholly a question of fact which the jury have the exclusive right to decide.

How sure must the jury be? This is, again, a matter of law which the court explains. In order to convict a defendant on any crime, the jury must be convinced of his guilt "beyond a reasonable doubt." That is a severe requirement. It is made so, in order to protect the innocent. In civil cases, where only money is at stake and not liberty or life, a jury decides by the district attorney to have the "weight of evidence" on his side. He must prove the State's case beyond a reasonable doubt.

The Verdict – The jury is now locked up in a jury room to debate the evidence and seek to agree on a verdict. All jurors must agree in order to bring in a verdict. Sometimes, they are kept out for a day or more if there is any chance of agreement. One stubborn juror may prevent a verdict, and his fellow jurymen take turns in trying to change his mind. If they are utterly unable to agree, the foreman so announces and the court dismisses the jury, and the whole trial goes for nought. This is called a "hung jury." The district attorney can begin all over again with a new jury, but his chances of success in a second trial are not good.

In a few States the old rule has been modified so that eleven or even seven jurors may bring in a verdict. This change prevents "hung juries," but its justice has yet to be approved generally.

In our case, let us assume that the jury has been so impressed by the evidence of the neighbor that it has serious doubts of the defendant's guilt even though the circumstantial evidence is strong. It, therefore, brings in a verdict of "Not guilty." The defendant is freed at once, and he is free for all time as he can never be tried again for the same crime, once a verdict of "Not guilty" has been reached.

Appeal – Had he been found guilty, his lawyer could have appealed to a higher court of the State (usually called the Supreme Court or the Court of Appeals) and obtained a review of the legal points involved. Generally speaking, questions of fact cannot be raised on appeal.

Constitutional Points – It is on such an appeal that constitutional questions often arise. The safeguards which surround every defendant in an American trial for crime should be observed by the trial judge; but if he fails to do his duty, their protection can still be obtained on appeal and the whole conviction set aside.

These are the main points:

1. There must be indictment by a grand jury in the case of any felony.
2. No person shall be tried again for the same crime after acquittal.
3. No person shall be compelled to be a witness against himself.
4. A defendant is entitled to a speedy and public trial by an impartial jury.
5. He must be informed of the nature of the accusation, be confronted by the witnesses against him, have the right to have witnesses summoned in his behalf, and have the assistance of counsel.
6. No *ex-post-facto* (i.e. "after the fact") law shall be passed, that is, a law making an act, done in the past, a crime.

The first five of these you will find in the Fifth and Sixth Amendments to the national Constitution; the sixth in Article I, Section 9, Paragraph 3. There are similar rules in all the State constitutions. They represent the results of the long fight for fair trials won by Englishmen before our republic was founded. They are part of the English common law from which our American legal system was developed.

Sentence and Punishment – The court sentences a convicted defendant after taking into view all the facts of his past life. Sometimes, in the case of first offenses for lesser crimes, a judge suspends sentence altogether. For almost all crimes, the term of imprisonment is fixed by the law within limits – from five to ten years, for instance. The judge decides whether the full term shall be imposed or less.

The view is now gaining ground that we should make more effort to reform our criminals. The old tortures and cruel punishments have long been abolished. No punishment is for revenge in our modern view. The object is to restrain the criminal from repeating his crime and also, by the example, to prevent others from committing the same crime. Sadly, the attempt to run prisons as reform schools has largely proven itself to be a failure, since the number of repeat offenders is still very high in our prison systems. In addition, our nation is paying a very high price for the experiment of warehousing men and women in prisons who are guilty of capital crimes, such as murder and kidnapping.

Many States are now introducing an "indeterminate sentence" as one aid to reform. This system allows a greater chance for individual treatment. A minimum term is fixed by law; beyond that it depends on how the prisoner behaves in prison; and after he is released he is "on parole" for a period, this meaning that if he does not behave as he promises, he goes back to prison to serve out his term. Perhaps the best type of reform that has been introduced in some courts involves the requirement of the criminal to pay restitution to his victim(s) in the form of money or labor after he has been released.

Children's Court – As part of this new wisdom in dealing with criminals, the children's or juvenile court has come into being, which handles cases involving children usually under 18 years of age. One of the worst features of the old system was that it threw all prisoners together, old and young, first offenders and hardened criminals. The result was that our jails trained all prisoners in corruption.

The juvenile court takes all cases of alleged crime up to eighteen years of age in some States. It is not run at all like the court we have described. The theory is that boys or girls of this age are not real criminals at heart, no matter what they have done. Every effort is made to appeal to their good side and turn them onto the right road again. However, the Bible commands the courts of law to administer justice in such a way that it does not become a respecter of persons. It is interesting to note that a growing number of courts are beginning to treat minors as adults in instances where their crimes are particularly heinous.

The judge hears the case without any jury, and the punishment is entirely in his hands. He is more like a just father than a court. Imprisonment is used as a last resort; and then a sentence is given only to a reform school, until the person is twenty-one. Most children are released on parole in the charge of a man or woman known as a probation officer. This officer goes to their homes and schools to watch over them. At regular intervals they report to the judge. As you can imagine, all of these special services are very costly. However, many people believe that this approach is less costly than having to deal with young people who grow up to be career criminals.

3. Civil Trials

General Description – Civil trials resemble criminal trials with the differences noted before. There is no district attorney, each side having its own lawyer. Either side can demand a jury if the case involves a considerable sum of money. But, many cases are left to the judge to decide, facts as well as law. The same rules of evidence apply, and lawyers for plaintiff and defendant present their cases in much the same order.

Pleadings – There being no crime charged, there is no indictment. There are, instead, pleadings between the two parties. The plaintiff serves a summons and also a complaint on the defendant, stating on what facts he makes his claim and how large of damages he claims. The defendant serves an answer in which he states his defense against the claims.

Judgment – If the plaintiff wins, he gets a judgment ordering the defendant to pay him a certain sum of money. This judgement, the court enforces through the sheriff who can seize property of the defendant and sell it, if necessary, to pay the judgment. In certain cases, also, a court issues an injunction; that is, an order directing the defendant to do something else other than pay money by way of reparation, or to refrain from doing something that is injuring or will injure the plaintiff. This is called "equity" relief, as distinct from "law" relief, which gives only money damages.

More than a century ago, a defendant who would not or could not pay a judgment was thrown into jail, to remain indefinitely. This was harsh, unjust and very stupid, for while in jail no debtor could possibly earn money to pay what he owed. Imprisonment for debt has now been abolished everywhere. You can read Dickens's novel, *Little Dorrit* and learn more about the tragedy and injustice of this old-time practice. Amy Dorrit was born and brought up in a London prison where her father was confined for debt. This novel had much to do with changing the law in England.

4. Common and Statute Law

Statute Law – You may have seen the huge volumes of laws which legislatures of every State have passed. One or two volumes are passed every year. These are called the "statute law," which simply means law enacted by a legislature.

Common Law. – We have also, a large and most important body of law which was never, thus, enacted by any legislature. It is called "common law," which means that it originated as common usage. That is the way all English law began, by the courts enforcing the general customs and moral laws of godly people who were seeking to live an orderly and peaceful life. Because England was a nation that was profoundly influenced by the principles of Biblical law, many of the general rules that developed were consistent with the Ten Commandments. Gradually, general rules developed which all the judges followed. It is of ancient origin and was taken over, in full, by our colonies when they split from England. This law is contained in the decisions of judges, and in the higher law of the Bible, and it is still growing as our courts interpret old laws.

This system makes our laws flexible, more easily bent to meet new necessities. It also makes for justice, since so many of our laws are the slow growth of many centuries of custom and experience; rather than, the opinions of any group of men. Most importantly, American common law is based upon the assumption that the laws contained in the Bible exhibit the purest and highest standard for determining what is just in the civil and moral realm. It should be clearly understood that common law cannot be properly administered by judges who are ignorant of, or indifferent to, Biblical principles.

Questions on the Text

Section 1

1. Against whom is a civil wrong done and against whom is a crime committed?
2. What are the parties to a suit?
3. What does the plaintiff seek to get in a civil suit?
4. Who is the plaintiff in a criminal suit?
5. Who is the lawyer for the plaintiff in a criminal trial?
6. What is a fine and why is it imposed?

Section 2

7. What does the coroner do?
8. When can the police make an arrest and when can a private citizen?
9. How does a district attorney secure a warrant for a man's arrest?
10. What are the prisoner's rights when arrested?
11. Up to what point is a man presumed to be innocent?
12. What is a writ of *habeas corpus*?
13. How does the Constitution protect it, and when may it be suspended?
14. What cases can a justice of the peace try?
15. Describe an arraignment.
16. What is bail and who can give it?
17. What evidence does a grand jury hear, and what does its indictment do?
18. How does the grand jury protect the innocent?
19. How can a defendant plead in a criminal trial?
20. What is a subpoena and why must it be obeyed?
21. Could any part of a trial be held in secret or without the defendant being present?
22. What does the trial jury do and of how many members does it consist?
23. How is it chosen?
24. What are talesmen and what are challenges?
25. What does a witness swear to do?
26. What is the crime of swearing falsely called?
27. Why is a witness allowed only to answer questions and not volunteer anything?
28. Why are there rules of evidence?
29. Can you give an example of hearsay?
30. What is direct examination and what is cross examination?
31. What is circumstantial evidence?
32. What is an alibi?
33. May a defendant testify in his own behalf? Must he?
34. What is the judge's charge and what does it contain?
35. What questions are left entirely to the jury to decide?
36. In what cases must a jury be convinced beyond a reasonable doubt?
37. What are the two verdicts that a jury may bring in?
38. What happens if a jury cannot agree?
39. Do all States require all twelve jurors to agree in order to bring a verdict?

40. What kind of questions are raised on appeal?
41. What are the six chief protections insured a defendant in a criminal suit by the Constitution?
42. What is prison reform and how does an indeterminate sentence operate?
43. Why were children's courts created?
44. Describe how they are conducted?
45. When a prisoner is released on parole what happens?

Section 3

46. How does a civil trial differ from a criminal trial?
47. Must there be a jury in a civil trial?
48. What does a judgment give a successful plaintiff?
49. How does an injunction differ from a judgment for money damages?
50. Can a man be imprisoned for debt?

Section 4

51. What is the distinction between common and statute law?

Questions for Discussion

1. What civil wrongs can you name?
2. What crimes can you name?
3. Why should one obey the law?
4. Have you ever seen a court-room or witnessed a trial?
5. What other kinds of evidence are apt to be deceptive besides hearsay? How about testimony of a near relative or someone deeply interested?
6. If you were cross-examining a witness how would you try to trip him up?

Test 9

114

† †

"We have staked the whole future of American civilization, not upon the power of government, far from it. We have staked the future...upon the capacity of each and all of us to govern ourselves, to sustain ourselves, according to the Ten Commandments of God."

JAMES MADISON 1778

★ ★ ★ ★ ★ ★ ★ ★ ★ ★ ★ ★ ★ ★ ★ ★ ★ ★

James Madison
(1751 - 1836)

James Madison, the fourth President of the United States of America, has been hailed as "the father of the Constitution." "Knowing the sinfulness of human nature, and believing that all men who have power must be distrusted, he sought not only to limit the powers of central government but also to divide and balance those powers." * Unfortunately, he argued that there was no danger that the federal courts would be a threat to States' rights since their power "was small and limited."

Although Madison sought a strong national government, he was not a centralist, as were Gouverneur Morris and Alexander Hamilton. Madison's inclination toward a stronger federal government was prompted by the excessive influence of majority rule in the States, the attacks on property, and their irresponsible issuance of paper money (inflation) under the Articles of Confederation.

Madison gave up study for the ministry (he was a life-long Anglican/ Episcopalian) for one of the great political careers in American history. He was primarily educated at home, and then, studied at the College of New Jersey (Princeton) under Rev. John Witherspoon, the only clergyman to sign the Declaration of Independence.

In 1775, Madison was chosen to serve on the Orange County committee on Safety, and was a member of the Virginia House of Delegates and the Constitutional Convention in 1776. (He was one of the major forces in bringing about the Constitutional Convention.) From 1780 to 1783, and again in 1786, he served in the Continental Congress. He served in the U.S. House of Representatives from 1789 to 1797. Thomas Jefferson appointed Madison Secretary of State, a post he held from 1801 - 1809. He was elected the fourth president in 1808, and was the nation's chief executive from 1809 - 1817.

During the debates surrounding the ratification of the Constitution, Madison wrote many of the essays which were collected and published as *The Federalist Papers*.

Madison held firm views on religious liberty and the vitality of the Christian faith; he strongly opposed a state church. On the issue of the separation of church and state, he wrote, *"There is not a shadow of right in the general* (federal) *government to intermeddle with religion . . . This subject is, for the honor of America, perfectly free and unshackled. The government has no jurisdiction over it."*

*"Madison: Statesman, President and Framer of The Constitution." Archie P. Jones, *The Christian Educator*, Oct. 1985. Copyright 1986. PRF.

CHAPTER 19

The Making of the Constitution

The Critical Period – We are apt to think that the Revolution established the United States, and that after the dark days of Valley Forge and the other heroic hours of the War of Independence, all was smooth sailing. Nothing could be further from the truth. The Revolution won independence for the colonies and made possible a united America. But for six long years, from 1783 to 1789, it was touch and go whether such a union would be achieved or whether the States would break apart into separate and weak nations to drift into disorder and probable absorption by some foreign power.

Articles of Confederation – The trouble lay with the Articles of Confederation, adopted in 1777 and made effective in 1781, under which the States constituted not a firmly united nation but little more than a league. "A firm league of friendship" was the phrase used in the Articles. The Congress which it created, like the Continental Congress which it succeeded, had neither the power to raise an army nor the power to raise money by taxation. It could order the States to furnish troops and money, but it could not enforce its orders.

With the war over and the peace treaty signed in 1783, the States went from bad to worse. The jealousy of the several States, which had made a league the strongest union acceptable in 1777, led to quarrels between them. Congress, the only central authority created, having neither the executive nor judicial power to carry out the laws, had the authority to raise money by borrowing; but it had exhausted its credit and could not even find money to pay the soldiers who had fought and won the war. It was mobbed by a crowd of drunken soldiers in Philadelphia in 1783, and compelled to flee to Princeton, New Jersey. Commerce among the States was hampered by customs duties which, as separate States, they had the right to impose against one another. New York taxed firewood from Connecticut and farm produce from New Jersey.

Convention of 1787 – Clear-headed men throughout the Confederation realized the gathering danger and set about meeting it. By God's grace, the colonies possessed a group of political thinkers as able as any the world has ever produced. We owe an inestimable gratitude to the men who fought the War of Independence. However, we should be just as grateful for those extraordinary men who, after the freedom was won, erected the permanent structure of our government without which freedom must have perished.

At the call of Congress, a convention met in Philadelphia in May, 1787, for the purpose of meeting these known and growing evils. Twelve States, all except Rhode Island, responded to the call and sent delegates, fifty-five in all. These men assembled in Independence Hall on May 25 and there, in the same room in which the Declaration of Independence had been signed and issued to the world eleven years before, began their great labor.

Four of the delegates were men of genius: Washington, Hamilton, Madison, and Franklin. Washington was unanimously chosen president of the convention and, throughout the four long months of debate, dispute, and compromise, his nobility of character and unselfish devotion to the cause of union, again and again, saved the convention from break-up. At the very outset, he sounded the lofty note, which was to animate the convention. A delegate had advocated half-way measures of amendment as likely to be more popular. To this Washington replied:

> *It is too probable that no plan we propose will be adopted. Perhaps another dreadful conflict is to be sustained. If, to please the people, we offer what we ourselves disapproved, how can we afterward defend our work? Let us raise a standard to which the wise and the honest can repair; the event is in the hand of God.*

Franklin was eighty-one years of age, the oldest member of the convention. He had returned from his marvelously successful diplomatic labors in Paris in behalf of the Confederation, and brought a rare tact and practical wisdom to the convention.

Hamilton and Madison were among the younger men, being thirty and thirty-six, respectively. Hamilton was the more brilliant of the two and the more eloquent. But, it was Madison whose profound learning and balanced mind contributed most to the Constitution that was created, and he has rightly been termed the "Father of the Constitution."

After the Constitution was completed by the convention and while its adoption by the States was still in doubt, these two, Hamilton and Madison (aided by John Jay), wrote *The Federalist,* a series of articles expounding the Constitution and urging its adoption. This volume ranks with the greatest works on political theory of all time.

There were many other able men in the convention, all of whom contributed something to the final result. The sessions were held in secret so that delegates could be free to speak their minds, and the disputes that arose could be settled in the privacy of the convention. Serious disagreements existed; interests of different sections clashed gravely. It was only by infinite patience and generous compromise that agreement was finally reached—not a compromise of those principles of right and wrong which no man should ever compromise, but compromise of those personal opinions and selfish interests which a man should always stand ready to sacrifice to the public good.

Sources of the Constitution – In praising the masterly achievement of the great men of 1787, we must not mistake the nature of their labor and conceive that they invented a wholly new and untried system of government. Their achievement would have been far from masterly and would probably have lasted only a brief period if they had attempted any such experiment. What they did was to draw on all the experience and wisdom of the past (especially the experience of the thirteen States as recorded in their constitutions and the example of the Bible), taking those elements which had worked well. They adapted them to the needs of the new nation, invented new devices where it seemed necessary, and built a new and beautifully proportioned structure. In one sense, almost nothing was new in the Constitution; in another sense, it was wholly new.

The Great Compromise – The chief dispute in the convention came between the small and large States. The former naturally feared that if they entered a nation, they would be outvoted and overwhelmed. In the Congress of the Confederation, each State had one vote and a continuation of this system was put forward by the delegates from New Jersey, therefore known as the New Jersey plan. Connecticut, Delaware, and Maryland sided with this view.

The Virginia plan, supported chiefly by Massachusetts, Pennsylvania, and North Carolina, was largely the work of Madison, and it provided for a legislature of two houses, in both of which representation was to be according to population. This would have given the large States complete control.

Debate upon these two plans was prolonged, and bitter, and it was not until the delegates from Connecticut put forward a plan known as "the Connecticut compromise" that any hope of agreement appeared. In this scheme, the House of Representatives was to represent the people in proportion to population; the Senate was to represent the States, large and small having an equal representation. "Yes," said Franklin, "when a joiner wishes to fit two boards, he sometimes pares off a bit from both." This compromise, as you will recognize, was the system adopted in the Constitution. So important did the smaller States consider their equal representation in the Senate that change of this provision is prohibited save by consent of each State. (Art. V). It is the only part of the Constitution requiring unanimous consent of the States for its alteration.

After this difficult problem was settled and the small States placated, the Virginia plan was largely adopted in respect to other matters. The central government received ample authority to tax, to raise armies, to control commerce between States, received, indeed, all those powers the lack of which brought the Confederation to the verge of disaster.

Slavery – Opinion against slavery had not crystallized by 1787, and while the Northern States sought to prohibit the importation of slaves, the wish of the Southern States, in part, prevailed. The slave population was not large at this time and its evils and peril to the nation were not clearly foreseen. The main disputes relating to slavery were compromised. The one was whether slaves should be counted in figuring the representative of a State in Congress and also, in apportioning taxes. This was compromised by agreeing that for both purposes five slaves should count as three individuals (Art. I, Sec. 2, Par. 3). The question of the slave trade was compromised by providing that it should not be ended prior to 1808; that was for twenty years. (Art. I, Sec. 9, Par. 1).

The Presidency – The President was modeled to some extent on the British King, carefully modified to avoid any possibility of the tyranny which the colonists knew, to their sorrow, in George III. His powers were strictly limited; he was to be elected for a fixed term of four years. Now, at this time, the British Government was rapidly moving away from its old monarchial character through the development of the prime minister, the head of the British Cabinet. Nominally appointed by the King, but really the leader of the majority in the House of Commons, this officer was fast becoming the true executive power of the British Government. But this fact was not realized at the time our Constitution was made. Therefore, the Convention of 1787 paid no attention to the example of the prime minister in creating our President. Had it copied the prime minister instead of the King, our President would be elected by the House of Representatives and would hold office, not for a fixed term but only so long as a majority of the House supported him. This is called the "responsible cabinet" system and is the way England is governed today. The point is important because it marks a vital difference between our government and the English system.

The convention feared to trust the people to select a President and, therefore, invented the Electoral College, already referred to. It was one of the more novel features of the Constitution; it was praised by every one and opposed by none; and it failed completely, being overridden by the popular desire for direct election by the year 1800.

The Supreme Achievement – The supreme creation of the convention was the relation of the Constitution to the government. It was made the "supreme law of the land" (Art. VI, Sec. 2), and a Supreme Court was created to interpret it. (Art. III, Sec. 1 and Sec. 2). It was made binding not only upon the States and individuals, but upon the national government, executive, legislative, and judicial departments alike. Effective force was given to its binding character through the power of the Supreme Court to declare acts of Congress, which violated the Constitution unconstitutional. This was undoubtedly the plan of the convention and through the wisdom and courage of Chief Justice Marshall of the Supreme Court, it speedily became the accepted interpretation.

"The American Constitution," says James Bryce in *The American Commonwealth,* "is the living voice of the people." That is the accurate truth. The people speak through the Constitution; and the Constitution, by its own provisions, is supreme above every other power in the country.

This was a magnificent conception and a wholly novel one. No other country in the world had a like system. It was the crowning achievement of a great labor because it established a society in which no individual was above the law.

Adoption of Constitution – Some one has remarked that our Constitution can be read through in about twenty-three minutes. It is very brief for the vast ground it covers and the amazing structure it rears. Yet, it took four months of the hardest labor to build it, and its completion marked perhaps the mightiest creation ever accomplished by any single group of men. There was deep emotion when, on that September 17, Benjamin Franklin arose to state his reasons for signing the completed document. The spirit of generosity and practical wisdom that ruled the convention breathed in his words:

120

I confess that there are several parts of this Constitution which I do not at present approve, but I am not sure I shall never approve them. For, having lived long, I have experienced many instances of being obliged, by better information or fuller consideration, to change opinions, even on important subjects, which I once thought right but found to be otherwise. It is therefore that, the older I grow, the more apt I am to doubt my own judgment, and to pay more respect to the judgment of others.

Thus I consent, sir, to this Constitution, because I expect no better, and because I am not sure that it is not the best. . . . I hope, therefore, that for our own sakes, as a part of the people, and for the sake of posterity, we shall act heartily and unanimously in recommending this Constitution wherever our influence may extend, and turn our future thoughts and endeavors to the means of having it well administered.

A unanimous vote of the States represented was cast for the Constitution. But it had to be referred to the States for ratification, and serious opposition arose in several States, including New York. Here it was that Hamilton and Madison did rare work. Their *Federalist* had much to do with winning New York. You can see the clear reasoning of these papers from the following quotation. It is from the 51st paper of the *Federalist,* probably written by Madison, and is a defense of the system of checks and balances of the Constitution with which you are already familiar:

Ambition must be made to counteract ambition. The interest of the man must be connected with the constitutional rights of the place. It may be a reflection of human nature that such devices should be necessary to control the abuses of government. But what is government itself but the greatest of all reflections on human nature. If men were angels, no government would be necessary. If angels were to govern men, neither external nor internal controls on government would be necessary. In framing a government which is to be administered by men over men, the great difficulty lies in this: you must first enable the government to control the governed; and in the next place oblige it to control itself.

On June 21, 1788, the Constitution was ratified by New Hampshire, the ninth State to do so, and therefore, under its terms (Art. VII), the Constitution went into effect. Virginia and New York followed close behind. But North Carolina held out until 1789, and Rhode Island until 1790. Meantime, the first presidential election had been held, in January, 1789; and on April 30, George Washington was inaugurated at Federal Hall, in New York City, as the first President of the United States.

The Growth of Nationalism. – Oddly enough, there was little dispute in the constitutional convention over the point that was to harass the country for seventy-five years, until settled for all time by the Civil War. That was the broad question of how firmly united the States were under the Constitution of 1789, whether, in fact, a true nation had been created, with ample power to perpetuate itself. As a matter of fact, the Convention of 1787, could not have gone farther than it did in creating a strong national government. The Constitution never would have been accepted by the States had our modern theory of nationalism been expressly adopted. It was necessary to leave the definition of this issue to coming generations, for each of the State leaders who originally signed the Constitution clearly assumed that they were voluntarily entering into a political alliance that could be dissolved.

In the gradual development of national powers, no American played a greater part than John Marshall, Chief Justice of the Supreme Court from 1801 to 1835. His name deserves to rank with the greatest names of the Convention of 1787, for it was his great intellect that gave life to their work and made a strong and united America possible. He stands with the greatest judges of any country, or any time. His work was not as noticeable as that of generals or Presidents, but it was not less vital to our national safety. Under his leadership, the Supreme Court upheld the liberal construction of the "elastic clause" (Art. I, Sec. 8, Par. 18) and prevented any encroachment by the States upon the powers essential to the preservation of the Union.

The railroads brought the different parts of the country closer together and aided the national spirit. The great movement to the West and the development of new States, without the old prejudices and traditions, made for unity. The War of 1812, and the war with Mexico strengthened patriotism and gave the national government new vigor.

The coming spirit of union in the country was never better stated than by Daniel Webster in his famous "Reply to Hayne," a speech delivered in the Senate in 1830. Senator Hayne, of South Carolina, had spoken in defense of the doctrine of States' rights and "nullification," that is, that a State had the right to nullify or set aside an act of Congress. The concluding words of Webster's speech were:

> When my eyes shall be turned to behold, for the last time, the sun in heaven, may I not see him shining on the broken and dishonored fragments of a once glorious Union; on States dissevered, discordant, belligerent; on a land rent with civil feuds, or drenched, it may be, with fraternal blood! Let their last feeble and lingering glance, rather, behold the gorgeous ensign of the republic, now known and honored throughout the earth, still full high advanced, its arms and trophies streaming in their original lustre, not a stripe erased or polluted, not a single star obscured, bearing for its motto no such miserable interrogatory as, 'What is all this worth?' Nor those other words of delusion and folly, 'Liberty first, and Union afterwards'; but everywhere, spread all over in characters of living light, blazing on all its ample folds, as they float over the sea and over the land, and in every wind under the whole heavens, that other sentiment, dear to every true American heart–'Liberty and Union, now and forever, one and inseparable!'

The land "drenched with fraternal blood" which Webster prophetically described came to pass in 1861, over the issue of secession, the right that the Southern States claimed to secede; that is, quit the Union. This was the culminating fight in the long dispute over the character of the federal government created in 1787. In his first inaugural, in 1861, President Lincoln defined his stand:

"I hold that in contemplation of universal law and of the Constitution the Union of these States is perpetual."

Sadly, politicians like Lincoln chose to establish their view of the Union at the point of a bayonet. The War Between the States has forced each generation of Americans to try to determine whether the United States is still based upon the principle that governments maintain their just powers only when they have the consent of the governed.

The victory for the Union ended this issue at the point of a gun. The final theory of the nation was expressed by the Supreme Court in the declaration that ours is "an indestructible union of indestructible States."

"The Indestructible States" – Despite the victory for the principle of perpetual union, the need for the States exists as much today, as ever. Ours is still a double government. The question now is the practical one of how far it is wise to increase national governmental activities, since the point surely exists at which the States will lose their self-respect and their efficiency as self-governing units. Home rule is still a vital principle of our government, as we have seen. It is a vital faith in America that the States must be preserved in full force and power. Events have necessarily increased the duties of the national government. It is the fear of many that the point has already been reached where the vigor of the States will be impaired by an overbearing national government. Those who believe in a strong national government feel that this is not so. It is not a question easily settled and it will, undoubtedly, fall to every reader of this book to help settle it. You must do so with a knowledge of our history and a clear understanding of the nature of our double government.

The Amendments – There are two methods of amending the Constitution provided: (1) by a convention called by Congress upon the application of the legislatures of two-thirds of the States (but amendments proposed by such a convention must, thereafter, be ratified by the legislatures or by conventions of three-fourths of the States, whichever Congress directs); and (2) by amendments proposed by a vote of two-thirds of both Houses and ratified by three-fourths of the States as under 1 (Art. V). The first method has never been used. Twenty-seven amendments have now been passed by the second method.

The first ten of these constitute the Bill of Rights and were adopted in 1791. The remaining seventeen amendments have been passed at various times over the years. It would be beneficial for you to study all of the constitutional amendments listed in the back section of this book.

Questions on the Text

1. What critical years followed the Revolution?
2. What were the chief weaknesses of the Articles of Confederation?
3. What taxes did New York impose on neighboring States?
4. Why was Congress moved from Philadelphia to Princeton in 1783?
5. Where did the convention of 1787 meet?
6. How many States sent delegates?
7. Who were the four leading figures of the convention?

8. What was *The Federalist*, who wrote it, and what was its purpose?
9. What were the sources of the Constitution?
10. What was the great compromise of the Constitution, what three States offered plans, and which State plan solved it?
11. Who was the author of the Virginia plan and to what extent did it prevail?
12. What were the two disputes over slavery and how were they compromised?
13. Upon what part of the British Government was the presidency modeled and with what differences?
14. How does the British Prime Minister differ from the President?
15. What is a responsible cabinet and how does it differ from the American cabinet?
16. Was the Electoral College a tried or an untried feature?
17. What was the crowning achievement of the convention of 1787?
18. What did James Bryce call the American Constitution?
19. What was Madison's argument for our system of checks and balances?
20. How serious was the opposition to the Constitution among the States and when was it ratified?
21. Why was the issue of nationalism not expressly settled in the Constitution?
22. Who was John Marshall and what service did he perform for our country?
23. What clause of the Constitution made the growth of nationalism possible?
24. What events aided the growth of a national spirit?
25. What was the doctrine of nullification and what right did the Southern States claim at the time of the Civil War?
26. What constitutional issue did the Civil War settle?
27. How was the relation of our national government to the States finally expressed by the Supreme Court?
28. Why are the States still vital to the success of our government?
29. What are the two methods of amending the Constitution and which alone has been used?
30. What amendments have been adopted since 1960? (See Appendix I)

Questions for Discussion

1. Do you know the names of any of the delegates to the convention of 1787 besides the four leaders?
2. If your State was one of the thirteen original States, what part did it play in the convention? Who represented it? What did they do, how did they vote, and when did your State ratify?
3. Do you think it was wise to hold the sessions of the convention in secret? What sort of body should meet in private?
4. When do you think it is right to compromise?
5. What other things bind the country together besides railroads?
6. In what respects is New York nearer to San Francisco today than New York was to Boston in 1789?
7. Are there any constitutional amendments now pending before Congress or before the States?

Test 10

CHAPTER 20

Your Government

The Voters to Come – The boys and girls of today are the voters of tomorrow. The government will be theirs to make it what they will. All the wisdom of the past, alone, cannot make a government successful. The fate of America rests with each generation. We have a wonderful machine, but it is only a machine, and it will run well or ill exactly as the voters direct. That is why it is the duty of every American to learn how his government works, to watch it, and to the utmost of his ability play his part in running it.

Change – Our Constitution provides for changes and it has been repeatedly changed in important particulars. It was the intention of the makers of our Constitution that it should be changed when occasion required. All that was insisted upon was that there should be time for reflection and that something more than a bare majority vote should be agreed. That must be our attitude today. We should respect our Constitution for its noble history and its great wisdom. We should reflect long before deciding to alter it. But if new conditions or new wisdom convince us that a change is needed, we should not hesitate to vote for it.

Socialism – There are few limits to the changes which the people of the nation could make in the Constitution if they saw fit. They could abandon our whole system of private ownership and establish a wholly socialistic state if they wished. That is, they could turn over all the means of production, land, factories, etc., to the state and let them be run cooperatively. The country has already turned over a few of our public utilities to the government to own and run. Some people think that more of such utilities should be owned by the government. Many others think not. The question is solely one of efficiency and justice and individual development. Will further socialistic steps produce the greatest good for the greatest number or not? The people have the power to decide and do whatever they think best. As soon as the bulk of the American people are convinced that the government should own and run all industry, they can change the Constitution to accomplish this goal. At present, the overwhelming majority of Americans prefer private ownership. They like the freedom and chance for individual success that it gives, the incentive it offers every one to develop and forge ahead. They have watched our experiments in government ownership and feel that government ownership of all industry would produce nothing less than national disaster. Most of the countries in Europe that have embraced socialism and big bureaucracies, have experienced nothing but horrible consequences on the political, social, and economic levels.

Communism – The only real limits upon our government are that it could not be made a government of riot or government by classes. In the course of the Russian Revolution, the Bolshevist government, for a time, held power by force. The theory seemed to be that the Bolshevist leaders knew better what the people wanted than the people themselves and, therefore, were justified in imposing their ideas upon the nation by whatever tyranny and bloodshed were necessary.

Communism is a backward and primitive system by comparison with our highly developed republic, and to attempt to introduce it in America would be to overturn our whole Constitution and government and destroy the progress of centuries.

That is one sort of government that could not be conducted under our Constitution by any process of amendment. Orderly compliance with law and with the will of the majority are the foundation of our whole system. Destroy that foundation and you destroy America. With it, you would destroy the greatest system man has ever devised to insure liberty and fair play to all.

National-State Relations: An Overview

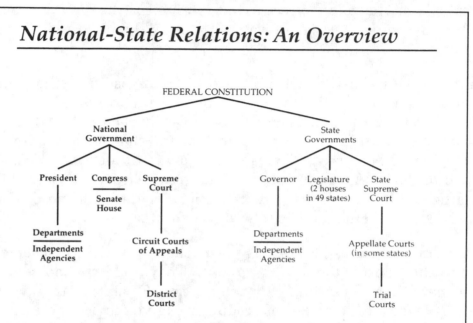

Under the U.S. Constitution, the nation is a federal republic that splits governing powers between the National Government and the states. The National, or Federal, Government is organized into three branches: Executive, Legislative and Judicial. The President heads the Executive Branch and carries out the laws passed by the bicameral Congress, the Legislative Branch made up of the Senate and House of Representatives. The court system, headed by the Supreme Court, makes up the Judicial Branch and interprets the laws.

The U.S. Supreme Court has the final authority in any disputes, such as Constitutional issues or treaties, between the states and the Federal Government. States also cannot prevent the Federal Government from exercising its powers under the Constitution. However, the states do retain powers as specified in the 10th amendment, one of the group of 10 amendments known as the Bill of Rights: "The powers not delegated to the United States by the Constitution, nor prohibited by it to the States, are reserved to their States respectively, or to the people."

The Federal Government depends on the states for two major responsibilities: approving amendments to the U.S. Constitution and election of federal officials. Amendments must be proposed by a two-thirds vote of both houses of Congress and ratified by three-fourths of state legislatures or special conventions. Subject to some limitations, the states have the right to determine the voting ballot form, conduct the elections, and tabulate and certify election results.

State governments cooperate with the Federal Government in many ways, including the implementation of joint law enforcement programs to prevent and detect crime and the use of federal grants for specific purposes, such as transportation construction or safety programs. In Illinois, federal aid accounts for about one-quarter of total state revenues. Of the amount, more than 50 percent of federal reimbursements is for welfare expenditures.

Americans All - One source of difficulty for America has always been the assimilation of new immigrants. It is very important for all people in America to learn the language and customs of our nation, so that they can learn the rules of fair play and become active participants in the life of our nation.

We should not ask people to forget their past; our various ethnic heritages and cultures can be something of pride and joy to us. However, instead of emphasizing our diversity to the point that it divides us, we should concentrate on the unity of our common culture and history as Americans. If we are unable to transcend our ethnic diversity to participate in a common culture, our nation will cease to be a land of fair play. Instead, it may become a land of squabbling groups who are only concerned for their own interests, rather than looking out for the needs of America.

The truth is that America was planned for a nation of God-fearing, literate people. It gives fair play to all who know how to play the game. It is the duty of every newcomer to our shores to learn English, become naturalized, and become a full-fledged American, as soon as possible. It is the duty of all other Americans to help our new neighbors in every way we can. It is the special duty of Christians to be faithful witnesses for Christ to those around us, teaching both newcomers and older residents alike about Christ and His principles for our lives. Only as our people work together for the glory of God and the good of America, can our land of fair play reach its full promise of good-will to all.

📖 A Prayer for our Country 📖

Almighty God, Who has given us this good land for our heritage, we humbly beseech Thee that we may always prove ourselves a people mindful of Thy favor and glad to do Thy will. Bless our land with honorable industry, sound learning, and pure manners. Save us from violence, discord, and confusion; from pride and arrogancy and from every evil way. Defend our liberties and fashion into one united people the multitudes brought hither out of many kindreds and tongues. Endue with the spirit of wisdom those to whom in Thy Name we entrust the authority of government, that there may be justice and peace at home, and that through obedience to Thy law, we may show forth Thy praise among the nations of the earth.

In the time of prosperity fill our hearts with thankfulness, and in the day of trouble suffer not our trust in Thee to fail.

Through Jesus Christ our Lord. Amen.

APPENDIX

THE CONSTITUTION OF THE UNITED STATES

We the people of the United States, in order to form a more perfect union, establish justice, insure domestic tranquility, provide for the common defense, promote the general welfare, and secure the blessing of liberty to ourselves and our posterity, do ordain and establish this Constitution for the United States of America.

ARTICLE I

Section 1

All legislative powers herein granted shall be vested in a Congress of the United States, which shall consist of a Senate and House of Representatives.

Section 2

1.   The House of Representatives shall be composed of members chosen every second year by the people of the several States, and the electors in each State shall have the qualifications requisite for electors of the most numerous branch of the State legislature.

2.   No person shall be a representative who shall not have attained to the age of twenty-five years, and been seven years a citizen of the United States, and who shall not, when elected, be an inhabitant of the State in which he shall be chosen.

3.   Representatives and direct taxes shall be apportioned among the several States which may be included within this Union, according to their respective numbers, which shall be determined by adding to the whole number of free persons, including those bound to service for a term of years, and excluding Indians not taxed, three-fifths of all other persons. The actual enumeration shall be made within three years after the first meeting of the Congress of the United States, and within every subsequent term of ten years, in such manner as they shall by law direct. The number of representatives shall not exceed one for every thirty thousand, but each State shall have at least one representative; and until such enumeration shall be made, the State of New Hampshire shall be entitled to choose three, Massachusetts eight, Rhode Island and Providence Plantations one, Connecticut five, New York six, New Jersey four, Pennsylvania eight, Delaware one, Maryland six, Virginia ten, North Carolina five, South Carolina five, and Georgia three.

4.   When vacancies happen in the representation from any State, the executive authority thereof shall issue writs of election to fill such vacancies.

5.   The House of Representatives shall choose their speaker and other officers; and shall have the sole power of impeachment.

Section 3

1.   The Senate of the United States shall be composed of two senators from each State, chosen by the legislature thereof, for six years; and each senator shall have one vote.

2.   Immediately after they shall be assembled in consequence of the first election, they shall be divided as equally as may be into three classes. The seats of the senators of the first class shall be vacated at the expiration of the second year, of the second class at the expiration of the fourth year, and of the third class at the expiration of the sixth year, so that one third may be chosen every second year; and if vacancies happen by resignation, or otherwise, during the recess of the legislature of any State, the executive thereof may make temporary appointments until the next meeting of the legislature, which shall then fill such vacancies.

3.   No person shall be a senator who shall not have attained to the age of thirty years, and been nine years a citizen of the United States, and who shall not, when elected, be an inhabitant of that State for which he shall be chosen.

4.   The Vice President of the United States shall be President of the Senate, but shall have no vote, unless they be equally divided.

5.   The Senate shall choose their other officers, and also a president Pro tempore, in the absence of the Vice President, or when he shall exercise the office of President of the United States.

6.   The Senate shall have the sole power to try all impeachments. When sitting for that purpose, they shall be on oath or affirmation. When the President of the United States is tried, the chief justice shall preside: and no person shall be convicted without the concurrence of two-thirds of the members present.

7.   Judgment in cases of impeachment shall not extend further than to removal from office, and disqualification to hold and enjoy any office of honor, trust or profit under the United States: but the party convicted shall nevertheless be liable and subject to indictment, trial, judgment and punishment, according to law.

Section 4

1.   The times, places, and manner of holding elections for senators and representatives, shall be prescribed in each State by the legislature thereof; but the Congress may at anytime by law make or alter such regulations, except as to the places of choosing senators.

2.   The Congress shall assemble at least once in every year, and such meeting shall be on the first Monday in December, unless they shall by law appoint a different day.

Section 5

1.   Each House shall be the judge of the elections, returns and qualifications of its own members, and a majority of each shall constitute a quorum to do business; but a smaller number may adjourn from day to day, and may be authorized to compel the attendance of absent members, in such manner, and under such penalties as each House may provide.

2.   Each House may determine the rules of its proceedings, punish its members for disorderly behavior, and, with the concurrence of two-thirds, expel a member.

3.   Each House shall keep a journal of its proceedings, and from time to time publish the same, excepting such parts as may in their judgment require secrecy; and the yeas and nays of the members of either House on any question shall, at the desire of one-fifth of those present, be entered on the journal.

4.   Neither House, during the session of Congress, shall, without the consent of the other, adjourn for more than three days, nor to any other place than that in which the two Houses shall be sitting.

Section 6

1.   The senators and representatives shall receive a compensation for their services, to be ascertained by law, and paid out of the Treasury of the United States. They shall in all cases, except treason, felony and breach of the peace, be privileged from arrest during their attendance at the session of their respective Houses, and in going to and returning from the same; and for any speech or debate in either House, they shall not be questioned in any other place.

2.   No senator or representative shall, during the time for which he was elected, be appointed to any civil office under the authority of the United States, which shall have been created, or the emoluments whereof shall have been increased during such time; and no person holding any office under the United States shall be a member of either House during his continuance in office.

Section 7

1.   All bills for raising revenue shall originate in the House of Representatives; but the Senate may propose or concur with amendments as on other bills.

2.   Every bill which shall have passed the House of Representatives and the Senate, shall, before it become a law, be presented to the President of the United States; if he approve he shall sign it, but if not he shall return it, with his objections to that House in which it shall have originated, who shall enter the objections at large on their journal, and proceed to reconsider it. If after such reconsideration two-thirds of that House shall agree to pass the bill, it shall be sent together with the objections, to the other House, by which it shall likewise be reconsidered, and if approved by two-thirds

of that House, it shall become a law. But in all such cases the votes of both Houses shall be determined by yeas and nays, and the names of the persons voting for and against the bill shall be entered on the journal of each House respectively. If any bill shall not be returned by the President within ten days (Sundays excepted) after it shall have been presented to him, the same shall be a law, in like manner as if he had signed it, unless the Congress by their adjournment prevent its return, in which case it shall not be a law.

3.   Every order, resolution, or vote to which the concurrence of the Senate and House of Representatives may be necessary (except on a question of adjournment) shall be presented to the President of the United States; and before the same shall take effect, shall be approved by him, or being disapproved by him, shall be repassed by tow-thirds of the Senate and House of Representatives, according to the rules and limitations prescribed in the case of a bill.

Section 8

1.   The Congress shall have power to lay and collect taxes, duties, imposts and excises, to pay the debts and provide for the common defense and general welfare of the United States; but all duties, imposts and excises shall be uniform throughout the United States;

2.   To borrow money on the credit of the United States;

3.   To regulate commerce with foreign nations, and among the several States, and with the Indian tribes;

4.   To establish an uniform rule of naturalization, and uniform laws on the subject of bankruptcies throughout the United States;

5.   To coin money, regulate the value thereof, and of foreign coin, and fix the standard of weights and measures;

6.   To provide for the punishment of counterfeiting the securities and current coin of the United States;

7.   To establish post offices and post roads;

8.   To promote the progress of science and useful arts, by securing for limited times to authors and inventors and exclusive right to their respective writings and discoveries;

9.   To constitute tribunals inferior to the Supreme Court;

10.   To define and punish piracies and felonies committed on the high seas, and offenses against the law of the nations;

11. To declare war, grant letter of marque and reprisal, and make rules concerning captures on land and water;

12. To raise and support armies, but no appropriation of money to that use shall be for a longer term than two years;

13. To provide and maintain navy;

14. To make rules for the government and regulation of the land and naval forces;

15. To provide for calling forth the militia to execute the laws of the Union, suppress insurrections and repel invasions;

16. To provide for organizing, arming, and disciplining the militia, and for governing such part of them as may be employed in the service of the United States, reserving to the States respectively the appointment of the officers, and the authority of training the militia according to the discipline prescribed by Congress;

17. To exercise exclusive legislation in all cases whatsoever, over such district (not exceeding ten miles square) as may, by cession of particular States, and the acceptance of Congress, become the seat of the government of the United States, and to exercise like authority over all places purchased by the consent of the legislature of the State in which the same shall be, for the erection of forts, magazines, arsenals, dockyards, and other needful buildings; and

18. To make all laws which shall be necessary and proper for carrying into execution the foregoing powers, and all other powers vested by this Constitution in the government of the United States, or in any department or officer thereof.

Section 9

1. The migration or importation of such persons as any of the States now existing shall think proper to admit, shall not be prohibited by the Congress prior to the year one thousand eight hundred and eight, but a tax or duty may be imposed on such importation, not exceeding ten dollars for each person.

2. The privilege of the writ of habeas corpus shall not be suspended, unless when in cases of rebellion or invasion the public safety may require it.

3. No bill of attainder or ex post facto law shall be passed.

4. No capitation, or other direct, tax shall be laid, unless in proportion to the census or enumeration herein before directed to be taken.

5. No tax or duty shall be laid on articles exported from any State.

6. No preference shall be given by any regulation of commerce or revenue to the

ports of one State over those of another: nor shall vessels bound to, or from, one State be obliged to enter, clear, or pay duties in another.

7.   No money shall be drawn from the treasury, but in consequence of appropriations made by law; and a regular statement and account of the receipts and expenditures of all public money shall be published from time to time.

8.   No title of nobility shall be granted by the United States: and no person holding any office of the profit or trust under them, shall, without the consent of the Congress, accept of any present, emolument, office, or title, of any kind whatever, from any king, prince, or foreign State.

Section 10

1.   No State shall enter into any treaty, alliance, or confederation; grant letters of marque and reprisal; coin money; emit bills of credit; make anything but gold and silver coin a tender in payment of debts; pass any bill of attainder, ex post facto law, or law impairing the obligation of contracts, or grant any title of nobility.

2.   No State shall, without the consent of the Congress, lay any imposts or duties on imports or exports, except what may be absolutely necessary for executing its inspection laws: and the net produce of all duties and imposts laid by any State on imports or exports, shall be for the use of the treasury of the United States; and all such laws shall be subject to the revision and control of the Congress.

3.   No State shall, without the consent of Congress, lay any duty on tonnage, keep troops, or ships of war in time of peace, enter into any agreement or compact with another State, or with a foreign power, or engage in war, unless actually invaded, or in such imminent danger as will not admit of delay.

ARTICLE II

Section 1

1.   The executive power shall be vested in a President of the United States of America. He shall hold his office during the term of four years, and, together with the Vice President, chosen for the same term, be elected, as follows:

2.   Each State shall appoint, in such manner as the legislature thereof may direct, a number of electors, equal to the whole number of senators and representatives to which the State may be entitled in the Congress: but no senator or representative, or person holding an office of trust or profit under the United States, shall be appointed an elector.

The electors shall meet in their respective States, and vote by ballot for two persons, of whom one at least shall not be an inhabitant of the same State with themselves. And they shall make a list of all the persons voted for, and of the number of votes for each; which list they shall sign and certify, and transmit sealed to the seat of the government of the United States, directed to the President of the Senate. The President of the Senate shall, in the presence of the Senate and House of Representatives, open all the certificates, and the votes shall then be counted. The person having the greatest number of votes shall be the President, if such number be a majority of the whole number of electors appointed; and if there be more than on who have such majority, and have an equal number of votes, then the House of Representatives shall immediately choose by ballot one of them for President; and if no person have a majority, then from the five highest on the list the said House shall in like manner choose the President. But in choosing the President, the votes shall be taken by States, the representation from each State having one vote; a quorum for this purpose shall consist of a member or members from two-thirds of the States, and a majority of all the States shall be necessary to a choice. In every case, after the choice of the President, the person having the greatest number of votes of the electors shall be the Vice President. But if there should remain two or more who have equal votes, the Senate shall choose from them by ballot the Vice President.

3.   The Congress may determine the time of choosing the electors, and the day on which they shall give their votes; which day shall be the same throughout the United States.

4.   No person except a natural born citizen, or a citizen of the United States, at the time of the adoption of this Constitution, shall be eligible to the office of the President; neither shall any person be eligible to that office who shall not have attained to the age of thirty-five years, and been fourteen years a resident within the United States.

5.   In case of the removal of the President from office, or of his death, resignation, or inability to discharge the powers and duties of the said office, the same shall devolve on the Vice President, and the Congress may by law provide for the case of removal, death, resignation, or inability, both of the President and Vice President, declaring what officer shall then act as President, and such officer shall act accordingly, until the disability be removed, or a President shall be elected.

6.   The President shall, at stated times, receive for his services, a compensation, which shall neither be increased nor diminished during the period for which he shall have been elected, and he shall not receive within that period any other emolument from the United States, or any of them.

7.   Before he enter on the execution of his office, he shall take the following oath or affirmation:–"I do solemnly swear (or affirm) that I will faithfully execute the office of President of the United States, and will to the best of my ability, preserve, protect and defend the Constitution of the United States."

Section 2

1.   The President shall be the commander in chief of the army and navy of the United States, and of the militia of the several States, when called into the actual service of the United States; he may require the opinion, in writing, of the principal officer in each of the executive departments, upon any subject relating to the duties of their respective offices, and he shall have power to grant reprieves and pardons for offenses against the United States, except in cases of impeachment.

2.   He shall have power, by and with the advice and consent of the Senate, to make treaties, provided two-thirds of the senators present concur; and he shall nominate, and by and with the advice and consent of the Senate, shall appoint ambassadors, other public ministers and consuls, judges of the Supreme Court, and all other offices of the United States, whose appointments are not herein otherwise provided for, and which shall be established by law; but the Congress may by law vest the appointment of such inferior officers, as they think proper, in the President alone, in the courts of law or in the heads of departments.

3.   The President shall have power to fill up all vacancies that may happen during the recess of the Senate, by granting commissions which shall expire at the end of their next session.

Section 3

He shall from time to time give to the Congress information of the state of the Union, and recommend to their consideration such measures as he shall judge necessary and expedient; he may, on extraordinary occasions, convene both Houses, or either of them, and in case of disagreement between them with respect to the time of adjournment, he may adjourn them to such time as he shall think proper; he shall receive ambassadors and other public ministers; he shall take care that the laws be faithfully executed, and shall commission all the officers of the United States.

Section 4

The President, Vice President, and all civil officers of the United States, shall be removed from office on impeachment for, and conviction of treason, bribery, or other high crimes and misdemeanors.

ARTICLE III

Section 1

The judicial power of the United States shall be vested in one Supreme Court, and in such inferior courts as the Congress may from time to time ordain and establish. The judges, both of the Supreme and inferior courts, shall hold their offices during good behavior, and shall, at stated times, receive for their services, a compensation, which shall not be diminished during their continuance in office.

Section 2

1.   The judicial power shall extend to all cases, in law and equity, arising under this Constitution, the laws of the United States, and treaties made, or which shall be made, under their authority;–to all cases affecting ambassadors, other public ministers and consuls;–to all of admiralty and maritime jurisdiction;–to controversies to which the United States shall be a party;–to controversies between two or more States;–between a State and citizens of another State;–between citizens of different States,–between citizens of the same State claiming land under grants of different States, and between a State, or the citizens thereof, and foreign States, citizens or subjects.

2.   In all cases affecting ambassadors, other public ministers and consuls, and those in which a State shall be party, the Supreme Court shall have original jurisdiction. In all the other cases before mentioned, the Supreme Court shall have appellate jurisdiction, both as to law and fact, with such exceptions, and under such regulations as the Congress shall make.

3.   The trial of all crimes, except in cases of impeachment, shall be by jury; and such trial shall be held in the State where the said crimes shall have been committed within any State, the trial shall be at such place or places as the Congress may by law have directed.

Section 3

1.   Treason against the United States, shall consist only in levying war against them, or in adhering to their enemies, giving them aid and comfort. No person shall be convicted of treason unless on the testimony of two witnesses to the same overt act, or on confession in open court.

2.   The Congress shall have power to declare the punishment of treason, but no attainder of treason shall work corruption of blood, or forfeiture except during the life of the person attained.

ARTICLE IV

Section 1

Full faith and credit shall be given in each State to the public acts, records, and judicial proceedings of every other State. And the Congress may by general laws prescribe the manner in which such acts, records and proceedings shall be proved, and the effect thereof.

Section 2

1.   The citizens of each State shall be entitled to all privileges and immunities of citizens in the several States.

2.   A person charged in any State with treason, felony, or other crime, who shall flee from justice, and be found in another State, shall on demand of the executive authority of the State form which he fled, be delivered up to be removed to the State having jurisdiction of the crime.

3.   No person held to service or labor in one State, under the laws thereof, escaping into another, shall in consequence of any law or regulation therein, be discharged from such service or labor, but shall be delivered up on claim of the party to whom such service or labor may be due.

Section 3

1.   New States may be admitted by the Congress into this Union; but no new State shall be formed or erected within the jurisdiction of any other State; nor parts of States, without the consent of the legislatures of the States concerned as well as of the Congress.

2.   The Congress shall have power to dispose of and make all needful rules and regulations respecting the territory or other property belonging to the United States; and nothing in this Constitution shall be so construed as to prejudice any claims of the United States, or of any particular State.

Section 4

The United States shall guarantee to every State in this Union a republican form of government, and shall protect each of them against invasion; and on application of the legislature, or of the executive (when the legislature cannot be convened) against domestic violence.

ARTICLE V

The Congress, whenever two-thirds of both Houses shall deem it necessary, shall propose amendments to this Constitution, or, on the application of the legislatures of two-thirds of the several States, shall call a convention for proposing amendments, which, in either case, shall be valid to all intents and purposes, a part of this Constitution when ratified by the legislatures of three-fourths of the several States, or by conventions in three-fourths thereof, as the one or the other mode of ratification may be proposed by the Congress; Provided that no amendment which may be made prior to they year one thousand eight hundred and eight shall in any manner affect the first and fourth clauses in the ninth section of the first article; and that no State, without its consent, shall be deprived of its equal suffrage in the Senate.

ARTICLE VI

1.   All debts contracted and engagements entered into, before the adoption of this Constitution, shall be as valid against the United States under this Constitution, as under the Confederation.

2.   This Constitution, and the laws of the United States which shall be made in pursuance thereof; and all treaties made, or which shall be made, under the authority of the United States, shall be the supreme law of the land; and the Judges in every State shall be bound thereby, anything in the Constitution or laws of any State to the contrary notwithstanding.

3.   The senators and representatives before mentioned, and the members of the several State legislatures, and all executive and judicial offices, both of the United States and of the several States, shall be bound by oath or affirmation to support this Constitution; but no religious test shall ever be required as a qualification to any office or public trust under the United States.

ARTICLE VII

The ratification of the conventions of nine States shall be sufficient for the establishment of this Constitution between the States so ratifying the same.

Done in Convention by the unanimous consent of the States present the seventeenth day of September in the year of our Lord one thousand seven hundred and eighty-seven, and of the independence of the United States of America the twelfth. In witness whereof we have hereunto subscribed our names,

New Hampshire
John Langdon
Nicholas Gilman

Massachusetts
Nathaniel Gorham
Rufus King

Connecticut
William Samuel Johnson
Roger Sherman

New York
Alexander Hamilton

New Jersey
William Livingston
William Patterson
David Brearley
Jonathan Dayton

Pennsylvania
Benjamin Franklin
Robert Morris
Thomas Fitzsimons
James Wilson
Thomas Mifflin
George Clymer
Jared Ingersoll
Gouverneur Morris

Delaware
George Read
John Dickinson
Jacob Broom
Gunning Bedford, Jr.
Richard Bassett

Maryland
James McHenry
Daniel Carroll
Daniel of St. Thomas Jenifer

Virginia
John Blair
James Madison, Jr.

North Carolina
William Blount
Hugh Williamson
Richard Dobbs Spaight

South Carolina
John Rutledge
Charles Cotesworth Pinckney
Charles Pinckney
Pierce Butler

Georgia
William Few
Abraham Baldwin

Attest:
William Jackson, Secretary

President and Deputy from Virginia, George Washington

Articles in addition to, and amendment of, the Constitution of the United States of America, proposed by Congress, and ratified by the legislatures of the several States, pursuant to the fifth article of the original Constitution.

ARTICLE I

Congress shall make no law respecting an establishment of religion or prohibiting the free exercise thereof; or abridging the freedom of speech, or of the press; or the right of the people peaceably to assemble, and to petition the government for a redress of grievances.

ARTICLE II

A well regulated militia, being necessary to the security of a free State, the right of the people to keep and bear arms, shall not be infringed.

ARTICLE III

No soldier shall, in time of peace, be quartered in any house, without the consent of the owner, nor in time of war, but in a manner to be prescribed by law.

ARTICLE IV

The right of the people to be secure in their persons, houses, papers and effects, against unreasonable searches and seizures, shall not be violated, and no warrants shall issue, but upon probable cause, supported by oath or affirmation, and particularly describing the place to be searched, and the persons or things to be seized.

ARTICLE V

No person shall be held to answer for a capital, or otherwise infamous crime, unless on a presentment or indictment of a grand jury, except in cases arising in the land or naval forces, or in the militia, when in actual service in time of war or public danger; nor shall any person be subject for the same offense to be twice put in jeopardy of life or limb; nor shall be compelled in any criminal case to be a witness against himself, nor be deprived of life, liberty, or property, without due process of law; now shall private property be taken for public use without just compensation.

ARTICLE VI

In all criminal prosecutions, the accursed shall enjoy the right to a speedy and public trial, by an impartial jury of the State and district wherein the crime shall have been committed, which district shall have been previously ascertained by law, and to be informed of the nature and cause of the accusation; to be confronted with the witnesses against him; to have compulsory process for obtaining witnesses in his favor, and to have the assistance of counsel for his defense.

ARTICLE VII

In suits at common law, where the value in controversy shall exceed twenty dollars, the right by trial by jury shall be preserved, and no fact tried by a jury shall be otherwise reexamined in any court of the United States, than according to the rules of the common law.

ARTICLE VIII

Excessive bail shall not be required, nor excessive fines imposed, nor cruel and unusual punishments inflicted.

ARTICLE IX

The enumeration in the Constitution, of certain rights, shall not be construed to deny or disparage others retained by the people.

ARTICLE X

The powers not delegated to the United States by the Constitution, nor prohibited by it to the States, are reserved to the States respectively, or to the people.

ARTICLE XI

The judicial power of the United States shall not be construed to extend to any suit in law or equity, commenced or prosecuted against one of the United States by citizens of another State, or by citizens or subjects of any foreign State.

ARTICLE XII

The electors shall meet in their respective States, and vote by ballot for President and Vice President, one of whom, at least, shall not be an inhabitant of the same State with themselves; they shall name in their ballots the person voted for as President, and in distinct ballots the person voted for as Vice President, and they shall make distinct lists of all persons voted for as President, and of all persons voted for as Vice President, and of the number of votes for each, which lists they shall sign and certify, and transmit sealed to the seat of the government of the United States, directed to the President of the Senate;—The President of the Senate, shall, in presence of the Senate and House of Representatives, open all the certificates and the votes shall then be counted;—The person having the greatest number of votes for President, shall be the President, if such number be a majority of the whole number of electors appointed; and if no person have such majority, then from the persons having the highest numbers not exceeding three on the list of those voted for as President, the House of Representatives shall choose immediately, by ballot, the President. But in choosing the President, the votes shall be taken by States, the representation from each State having one vote; a quorum for this purpose shall consist of a member or members from two-thirds of the States, and majority of all the States shall be necessary to a choice. And if the House of Representatives shall not choose a President whenever the right of choice shall devolve upon them, before the fourth day of March next following, then the Vice President shall act as President, as in the case of the death or other constitutional disability of the President. The person having the greatest number of votes as Vice President shall be the Vice President, if such number be a majority of the whole number of electors appointed and if no person have a majority, then from the two highest numbers on the list, the Senate shall choose the Vice President; a quorum for the purpose shall consist of two-thirds of the whole number of Senators, and a majority of the whole number shall be necessary to a choice. But no person constitutionally ineligible to the office of President shall be eligible to that of Vice President of the United States.

ARTICLE XIII

Section 1

Neither slavery nor involuntary servitude, except as punishment for crime whereof the party shall have been duly convicted shall exist within the United States, or any place subject to their jurisdiction.

Section 2

Congress shall have power to enforce this article by appropriate legislation.

ARTICLE XIV

Section 1

All persons born or naturalized in the United States, and subject to the jurisdiction thereof, are citizens of the United States and of the State wherein they reside. No State shall make or enforce any law which shall abridge the privileges or immunities of citizens of the United States; nor shall any State deprive any person of life, liberty, or property, without due process of law; nor deny to any person within its jurisdiction the equal protection of the laws.

Section 2

Representatives shall be apportioned among the several States according to their respective numbers, counting the whole number of persons in each State, excluding Indians not taxed. But when the right to vote at any election for the choice of electors for President and Vice President of the United States, representatives in Congress, the executive and judicial officers of a State, or the members of the legislature thereof, is denied to any of the male inhabitants of such State, being twenty-one years of age, and citizens of the United States or in any way abridged, except for participation in rebellion, or other crime, the basis of representation therein shall be reduced in the proportion which the number of such male citizens shall bear to the whole number of male citizens twenty-one years of age in such State.

Section 3

No person shall be a senator or representative in Congress, or elector of President and Vice President, or hold any office, civil or military under the United States, or under any State, who, having previously taken an oath, as a member of Congress, or as an officer of the United States, or as a member of any State legislature, or as an officer executive or judicial officer of any State, to support the Constitution of the United States, shall have engaged in insurrection or rebellion against the same, or given aid or comfort to the enemies thereof. But Congress may, by vote of two-thirds of each House, remove such disability.

Section 4

The validity of the public debt of the United States, authorized by law, including debts incurred for payment of pensions and bounties for services in suppressing insurrection or rebellion, shall not be questioned. But neither the United States nor any State shall assume or pay any debt or obligation incurred in aid of insurrection or rebellion against the United States, or any claim for the loss or emancipation of any slave; but all such debts, obligations and claims shall be held illegal and void.

Section 5

The Congress shall have power to enforce, by appropriate legislation, the provisions of this article.

ARTICLE XV

Section 1

The right of citizens of the United States to vote shall not be denied or abridged by the United States or by any State on account of race, color, or previous condition of servitude.

Section 2

The Congress shall have power to enforce this article by appropriate legislation.

ARTICLE XVI

The Congress shall have power to lay and collect taxes on incomes, from whatever source derived, without apportionment among the several States, and without regard to any census or enumeration.

ARTICLE XVII

The Senate of the United States shall be composed of two senators form each State, elected by the people there of, for six years; and each senator shall have one vote. The electors in each State shall have the qualification requisite for electors of the most numerous branch of the State legislature.

When vacancies happen in the representation of any State in the Senate, the executive authority of such State shall issue writs of election to fill such vacancies: Provided, That the legislature of any State may empower the executive thereof to make temporary appointments until the people fill the vacancies by election as the legislature may direct.

This amendment shall not be so construed as to affect the election or term of any senator chosen before it becomes valid as part of the Constitution.

ARTICLE XVIII

Section 1

After one year from the ratification of this article the manufacture, sale, or transportation of intoxicating liquor within, the importation thereof into, or the exportation thereof from the United States and all territory subject to the jurisdiction thereof for beverage purposes is hereby prohibited.

Section 2

The Congress and the several States shall have concurrent power to enforce this article by appropriate legislation.

Section 3

This article shall be inoperative unless it shall have been ratified an an amendment to the Constitution by the Legislatures of the several States, as provided in the Constitution, within seven years from the date of the submission hereof to the States by the Congress.

ARTICLE XIX

The right of the citizens of the United States to vote shall not be denied or abridged by the United States or by any State on account of sex.

Congress shall power to enforce this article by appropriate legislation.

ARTICLE XX

Section 1

The terms of the President and Vice President shall end at noon on the 20th day of January, and the terms of Senators and Representatives at noon on the 3rd day of January, of the years in which such terms would have ended if this article had not been ratified; and the terms of their successors shall then begin.

Section 2

The Congress shall assemble at least once in every year, and such meeting shall begin at noon on the 3rd day of January, unless they shall by law appoint a different day.

Section 3

If, at time fixed for the beginning of the term of the President, the President elect shall have died, the Vice President elect shall become President. If a President shall not have been chosen before the time fixed for the beginning of his term, or if the

President elect shall have failed to qualify, the the Vice President elect shall act as President until a President shall have qualified; and the Congress may by law provide for the case wherein neither a President elect nor a Vice President elect shall have qualified, declaring who shall then act as President , or the manner in which one who is to act shall be selected, and such person shall act accordingly until a President or Vice President shall have qualified.

Section 4

The Congress may by law provide for the case of the death of any of the persons from whom the House of Representatives may choose a President whenever the right of choice shall have devolved upon them, and for the case of the death of any of the persons from whom the Senate may choose a Vice President whenever the right of choice shall have devolved upon them.

Section 5

Sections 1 and 2 shall take effect on the 15th day of October following the ratification of this article.

Section 6

This article shall be inoperative unless it shall have been ratified as an amendment to the Constitution by the legislatures of three-fourths of the several States within seven years from the date of its submission.

ARTICLE XXI

Section 1

The eighteenth article of amendment to the Constitution of the United States is hereby repealed.

Section 2

The transportation or importation into any State, Territory, or possession of the United States for delivery or use therein of intoxicating liquors, in violation of the laws thereof, is hereby prohibited.

Section 3

This article shall be inoperative unless it shall have been ratified as an amendment to the Constitution by conventions in the several States, as provided in the Constitution, within seven years from the date of the submission hereof to the States by the Congress.

ARTICLE XXII

Section 1

No person shall be elected to the office of the President more than twice, and no person who has held the office of the President, or acted as President, for more than two years of a term to which some other person was elected President shall be elected to the office of the President more than once. But this Article shall not apply to any person holding the office of President when this Article was proposed by the Congress, and shall not prevent any person who may be holding the office of President, or acting as President, during the term within which this Article becomes operative from holding the office of President or acting as President during the remainder of such term.

Section 2

This article shall be inoperative unless it shall have been ratified as an amendment to the Constitution by the legislatures of three-fourths of the several States within seven years from the date of its submission to the States by the Congress.

ARTICLE XXIII

Section 1

The District constituting the seat of Government of the United States shall appoint in such manner as the Congress may direct:

A number of electors of President and Vice President equal to the whole number of Senators and Representatives in congress to which the District would be entitled if it were a State, but in no event more than the least populous State; they shall be in addition to those appointed by the States, but they shall be considered, for the purposes of the election of President and Vice President, to be electors appointed by a State; and they shall meet in the District and perform such duties as provided by the twelfth article of amendment.

Section 2

The Congress shall have power to enforce this article by appropriate legislation.

ARTICLE XXIV

Section 1

The right of citizens of the United States to vote in any primary or other election for President of Vice President, for electors for President or Vice President, or for Senator or Representative in Congress, shall not be denied or abridged by the United States or any State by reason of failure to pay any poll tax or other tax.

Section 2

The Congress shall have power to enforce this article by appropriate legislation.

ARTICLE XXV

Section 1

In case of the removal of the President from office or of his death or resignation, the Vice President shall become President.

Section 2

Whenever there is a vacancy in the office of the Vice President, the President shall nominate a Vice President who shall take office upon confirmation by a majority vote of both Houses of Congress.

Section 3

Whenever the President transmits to the President pro tempore of the Senate and the Speaker of the House of Representatives his written declaration that he is unable to discharge the powers and duties of his office, and until he transmits to them a written declaration to the contrary, such power and duties shall be discharged by the Vice President as Acting President.

Section 4

Whenever the Vice President and a majority of either the principal officers of the executive departments or of such other body as Congress may by law provide, transmit to the President pro tempore of the Senate and the Speaker of the House of Representatives their written declaration that the President is unable to discharge the powers and duties of his office, the Vice President shall immediately assume the powers and duties of the office as Acting President.

Thereafter, when the President transmits to the President pro tempore of the Senate and the Speaker of the House of Representatives his written declaration that no inability exists, he shall resume the powers and duties of his office unless the Vice President and a majority of either the principal officers of the executive department or of such other body as Congress may by law provide, transmit within four days to the President pro tempore of the Senate and the Speaker of the House of Representatives their written declaration that the President is unable to discharge the powers and duties of his office. Thereupon Congress shall decide the issue, assembling within forty-eight hours for that purpose if not in session. If the Congress, within twenty-one days after receipt of the latter written declaration, or, if Congress is not in session, within twenty-one days after Congress is required to assemble, determines by two-thirds vote of both Houses that the President in unable to discharge the powers and duties of his office, the Vice President shall continue to discharge the same as Acting President; otherwise, the President shall resume the powers and duties of his office.

ARTICLE XXVI

Section 1

The right of citizens of the United States, who are eighteen years of age or older, to vote shall not be denied or abridged by the United States or by any State on account of age.

Section 2

The Congress shall have power to enforce this article by appropriate legislation.

ARTICLE XXVII

No law, varying the compensation for the services of the senators and representatives, shall take effect, until an election of representatives shall have intervened.

NOTES:

1. The first ten Amendments, called the Bill of Rights were ratified December 15, 1791.
2. The Eleventh Amendment was ratified February 7, 1795; but was not declared until January 8, 1798.
3. The Twelfth Amendment was ratified June 15, 1804.
4. The Thirteenth Amendment was ratified December 6, 1865.
5. The Fourteenth Amendment was ratified July 9, 1868. This Amendment partly superseded Article I, Sec. 2, Par. 3.
6. The Fifteenth Amendment was ratified February 3, 1870
7. The Sixteenth Amendment was ratified February 3, 1913.
8. The Seventeenth Amendment was ratified April 8, 1913, in lieu of Art. I, Sec. 2, Par. 1 of the Constitution and so much of paragraph two of the same Section as relates to the filling of vacancies.
9. The Eighteenth Amendment was ratified in January 16, 1919. This Amendment was repealed by the Twenty-First Amendment December 5, 1933.
10. The Nineteenth Amendment was ratified August 18, 1920.
11. The Twentieth Amendment was ratified January 23, 1933.
12. The Twenty-First Amendment was ratified December 5, 1933.
13. The Twenty-Second Amendment was ratified February 27, 1951.
14. The Twenty-Third Amendment was ratified March 29, 1961.
15. The Twenty-Fourth Amendment was ratified January 23, 1964.
16. The Twenty-Fifth Amendment was ratified February 10, 1967.
17. The Twenty-Sixth Amendment was ratified July 1, 1971.
18. The Twenty-Seventh Amendment was ratified May 7, 1992. This particular amendment was originally proposed to the States by Congress on September 25, 1789, the same day as the Bill of Rights.

AMERICA'S CHRISTIAN HERITAGE

"We have this day restored the Sovereign to Whom all men ought to be obedient, and from the rising to the setting of the sun, let His kingdom come." **SAMUEL ADAMS July 4, 1776**

Samuel Adams
(1722 - 1803)

One of the foremost patriot-leaders in the struggle for the rights of men and the independence of the American colonies. Author of the *Massachusetts Resolves,* originator of the Committees of Correspondence which served to unite the colonies in their stand against Great Britain, organizer of the Boston Tea Party, Delegate to the Continental Congress (1774 - 1781), signer of the Declaration of Independence, Lt. Gov. and Gov. of Massachusetts (1789 - 1797).

Samuel Adams of Boston may rightly be called "*the father of The American War for Independence.*" He stands as a prime example of how strong, Christian character can have an impact upon a nation." . . . the austere purity of his life witnessed the sincerity of his profession. Evening and morning his house was a house of prayer. . . (his desire was) that 'Boston might become a Christian Sparta.'"[1] He was a "statesman of clear logical mind . . . [with a] will that resembled well-tempered steel, which may ply but will not break."[2]

Adams was pre-eminent among colonial leaders who demanded the right guaranteed them as Englishmen. "He had grasped the idea that the king, lords, and commons, as well as the colonies, were subject to the authority and bound by the limitations of constitutional law."[3]

When the violations of the colonists' rights by king and parliament grew more frequent and more oppressive, Adams became "the center around which all the movements of the patriots turned." He gave all of himself to the cause of freedom—his time, his labors, his zeal. Perhaps more than any other individual, he "breathed life into the American Revolution." Yet, with all his personal effort, Adams made it clear that he and all colonials must "rely not upon the arm of flesh but on the arm of that all-powerful God Who is able to unite this country as brothers in common cause."

One of Adams' chief concerns was that his American compatriots be able to "reason out their political convictions from the standpoint of their Christian rights," that they realize that only through mastery of Biblical principles, could they produce godly results.

"*The rights of the colonists,*" he wrote, "*may be best understood by reading and carefully studying the institutes of the great Law Giver and Head of the Christian Church, which are to be found clearly written and promulgated in the New Testament.*"

---

[1]George Bancroft, *History of the United States,* 1886. [2]idem. [3]Rosalie Slater *Teaching & Learning America's Christian History,* F.A.C.E. 1973. pp 250-258. Copyright 1986 PRF

God is Sovereign, Not Man

"For the Lord is our judge, the Lord is our lawgiver, the Lord is our king: He will save us" (Isaiah 33:22).

"And the people gave a shout, saying, 'It is the voice of a god, and not of a man'" (Acts 12:22), and Herod believed their words. The belief that those who rule are self-styled gods, independent of God's sovereignty over them, is the grand delusion for which Herod fell. God did not take long to remind King Herod that all rulers are subject to His sovereignty and law. An angel of the Lord struck him and he was eaten by worms and died, because he did not give God the glory (Acts 12:23).

Today, the United States finds herself in the midst of making a similar choice. It is true that our coins have "In God We Trust" stamped on them. But it is equally true that out nation puts more trust in the money itself than in the God who supplies all wealth. This nation is being warned, just as Israel was warned. God is reminding the United States that her prosperity and security do not come by way of the state. As Christians, we must heed God's warning that a forgetful nation is a doomed nation. Have we come to the place where we now believe that "My power and the strength of my hand made me this wealth" (Deuteronomy 8:17)? God's assessment of such presumption is not easy to take for an unrepentant nation:

> But you shall remember the Lord your God, for it is He who is giving you power to make wealth, that He may confirm His covenant which He swore to your fathers, as it is this day. And it shall come about if you ever forget the Lord your God, and go after other gods and serve them and worship them, I testify against you today that you shall surely perish. Like the nations that the Lord makes to perish before you, so you shall perish; because you would not listen to the voice of the Lord your God (Deuteronomy 8:18-20).

Herod saw himself as a god. But what is even more frightening, is that the people accepted him as a god. It is no less true today that people reject the God of the Bible and His faithful provisions of life, liberty, and property and turn to the state for sustenance and security. Where we are told to pray, "Our Father who art in heaven . . . Give us this day our daily bread" (Matthew 6:9, 11), we too often turn to the state for our daily bread. Where the Bible tells us that God is our Father, more often than not, the people make the government their father, because it can provide them all the financial aid they need.

This is why the First Commandment must be our starting point for the proper ordering of ourselves, our families, our churches, and our nation. We must never put any of man's laws before the First Commandment: "I am the Lord your God...you shall have no other gods before Me" (Exodus 20:2,3). Adherence to the first commandment protects us from those who would rewrite it to read "I, the state, am your God. You shall have no other gods before me." Therefore, the Biblical covenant structure may be stated as follows: (1) the absolute sovereignty of a transcendent God who is always present (immanent) with His people; (2) He sets up a hierarchy; (3) He lays down the law; (4) He judges men continually and also at the end of time, and (5) He preserves His kingdom.

When a ruler decrees either by words or deeds that he is independent of God's government, or that justice is defined according to his self-made laws, or that the people should look to the state for salvation, then God responds with judgement. A nation might not see God's judgment in the same way as Herod did, but time brings all things to light. Choosing man as the sovereign ruler, independent of God, will lead a nation to slavery and eventual destruction.

For the despot, power is all that matters. Words and what they mean, and what they can mean, are used to change opinions. When man makes up his own meaning on the basis of his own power, chaos results. Then a power struggle takes place among all those people who want their word to rule. This is the primary reason why so many of our important laws and constitutions are often being re-interpreted in a manner that is far removed from the original intent of the authors of such documents. Sinful men simply refuse to be bound by any code of law that restraints their lustful desire to be like gods.

Let us briefly look at some older definitions of the word "government" to see that it meant more than the civil government at the national level. The dictionary is always a good place to begin. Noah Webster's *An American Dictionary of the English Language* (first published in 1828) defines government this way:

> GOVERNMENT, *n.* Direction; regulation. "These precepts will serve for the *government* of our conduct."
> 2.   Control; restraint. "Men are apt to neglect the *government* of their temper and passions."
> 3.   The exercise of authority; direction and restraint exercised over the actions of men in communities, societies or states; the administration of public affairs, according to the established constitution, laws and usages, or by arbitrary edicts. "Prussia rose to importance under the *government* of Frederick II."
> 4.   The exercise of authority by a parent or householder. "Children are often ruined by a neglect of *government* in parents. Let family *government* be like that of our heavenly Father, mild, gentle and affectionate."

Did you notice the emphasis here? All human government begins with the *individual*. The Scriptures call this self-government or self-control (Galatians 6:23; Acts 24:25). Self-government undergirds all institutional governments, including the mothers and fathers in family government, elders in church government, and civil servants at all jurisdiction levels in civil government. Webster does not define government as the state and only the state.

Where did these early definers of government get these fundamental ideas?

152

From the Bible. When the Bible speaks of "government" in the singular, it refers to the government of Jesus Christ which encompasses all other governments:

> *For a child will be born to us, a son will be given to us; and the government will rest on His shoulders; and His name will be called Wonderful Counselor, Mighty God, Eternal Father, Prince of Peace. There will be no end to the increase of His government or of peace, on the throne of David and over His kingdom, to establish it and to uphold it with justice and righteousness from then on and forevermore. The zeal of the Lord of hosts will accomplish this (Isaiah 9:6,7).*

His government is as comprehensive as His creation. He created all things; He rules over all things.

The One Government of God

The word "government" has a comprehensive definition that includes self-government, family government, church government, and civil government. The operation of these plural governments (families, churches, and civil government at the local, county, State, and federal levels) is dependent upon the one government of God as expressed in Isaiah 9:6,7 and other passages. Jesus "upholds all things by the word of His power" (Hebrews 1:3) and "by Him all things were created, both in the heavens and on earth, visible and invisible, whether thrones or dominions or rulers or authorities – all things have been created by Him and for Him. And He is before all things, and in Him all things hold together" (Colossians 1:16, 17).

God then is the *model* for all types of governments. The created order *images* God. The study of the law given to individuals, families, churches, and nations will show that these divine directives reflect God's attributes. For example, the individual is to be holy as God is holy; the love that Jesus expressed in giving his life for the church is to be copied by husbands in their love for their wives (Ephesians 5:22-34); the discipline that fathers give their children is a model of God's discipline of His children (Hebrews 12:1-13); the state is God's "minister ... an avenger who brings wrath upon the one who practices evil" (Romans 13:4; cf 12:19).

How does the principle of the "many" governments work itself out in family, church, and state? Children are commanded to obey their parents in the Lord (Ephesians 6:1). There is real authority here and parents have jurisdiction within their own family structure.

Church members are part of a jurisdictional government called "ecclesiastical government." The church is given the "keys of the kingdom of heaven" and with these keys the leadership can "bind" and "loose" within the church (Matthew 16:19). The church has the authority to excommunicate unrepentant members (Matthew 18:15-18). The church also has the power to handle legal matters that many would see as the exclusive right of the state (1 Corinthians 6:1-11). The book of Hebrews exhorts us, "Obey your leaders, and submit to them; for they keep watch over your souls, as those who will give an account" (Hebrews 13:17). Ultimately, God will demand an accounting from all individuals regarding their obedience to the authorities, but this includes all authorities, not just civil authorities.

The state has the power of the sword: the civil government "does not bear the sword for nothing" (Romans 13:4). Because it has legitimate authority, Peter can write: "Submit yourselves for the Lord's sake to every human institution, whether to a king as the one in authority, or to governors as sent by him for the punishment of evildoers and the praise of those who do right" (1 Peter 2:13, 14).

The One and the Many

God has established three basic categories of authority for the proper ordering of society. Mothers and fathers have authority over their children (Proverbs 6:20, 21; 15:5; 30:17; Ephesians 6:1-3; Colossians 3:20). Church leaders, elders and deacons, hold authority in the church (Matthew 16:19; 18:15-20; 1 Thessalonians 5:12, 13; 1 Timothy 5:17, 18; Hebrews 13:17; 1 Peter 5:1-3). Civil rulers exercise political authority by God's decree (Matthew 22:21; Romans 13:1-7; 1 Peter 2:13, 14).

In other relationships, contracts can bind individuals and groups to the stipulations of those contracts. The employer-employee relationship is contractual and carries with it legitimate authority to enforce the obligations of the contract by punishing the contract-breaker and seeing to it that restitution is paid to contract-keeper. A contract is based upon God's covenantal design. God sets forth obligations, benefits for obeying the covenant, and reprisals for breaking covenant stipulations. Organizations can lawfully enforce contracts like God enforces His covenants.

The concept of multiple delegated authorities is patterned after the Divine One and Many – the Trinity. There is one God (Unity) and there are three Persons (Diversity) in the Godhead, each of whom is God. Each member of Trinity; Father, Son, and Holy Spirit, has authority to accomplish the one purpose and duty – obedience to God for His glory.

What, then, should be ultimate in society? The one or the many? Unity or diversity? The individual or the group? Should we have one monolithic authority or should every individual be an authority unto himself?

The creation reflects the Creator. We find it reflects God's unity and His diversity. In the creation, and in mankind's institutions, unity is not to swallow up diversity, and diversity is not to blow apart unity. Thus, we should expect to find that debates over the proper form of civil government always return to this theme: Which is primary, unity, or diversity? And the Biblical answer is simple in principle (though difficult to achieve in practice): *neither!*

What kind of political structures do anti-Christian civilizations recommend? They insist that god is not a Trinity. He is not simultaneously One and Many. He is not "three Persons, yet also One Person." They deny that there is equal ultimacy of the

154

One and the Many, meaning that the unity of God is not ultimate over the plurality of the Persons of the Trinity, each of Whom is God. They insist that God is either one or many, either unified or totally diverse. A nation's view of government reflects its view of God and God's legal relationships with mankind. So, governments recommended by anti-Christians tend either toward statism or anarchy, rule by one or the many.

Anarchy

One proposed solution to the problem of how power and authority ought to function in society is to place sovereignty totally with the individual. (Whenever we see the word "total" or "totally" with respect to man and his institutions, beware : tyranny is lurking in the shadows.) Anarchy is the ultimate implication of this philosophy: every man is his own judge and jury. However, the Bible tells us that God is man's ultimate Judge and Jury. God lays down the law. He places man and the creation under the restraining factor of His law. Furthermore, the Fall of man demonstrates the rebellion in the heart of man towards God's sovereignty and has made external restraint even more necessary.

The anarchist believes that external restraint, perpetuated by civil governments, are the culprits for all of our ills. The individual must work to remove the shackles of external restraint and open the floodgates of unbridled freedom for all people. For the anarchist, civil government is the enemy of society, simply because it rules over the individual. The word anarchy is made up of two Greek words, *a* which means "no" and *arche* which means "rule" or "power." An anarchist despises any power greater than himself and he will work in a violent way to overthrow any authority that works to curtail any of his individual freedoms, no matter how deviant or dangerous to the broader society.

Modern-day terrorism is a manifestation of anarchy under the guise of "freedom." The counter culture of the '60's fostered anarchy as a way of reversing the order of society. Much of the rock music fanned the flames of the '60's radicalism.

The revolutionary anarchist believes in the inherent goodness of *some* men, and that with an overthrow of the existing order and the death of the remaining evil men, a new society will emerge from the rubble. The pacifist anarchist (such as the Russian writer Tolstoy) believes in the innate evil of man's coercive institutions, and so withdraws from power, leaving those who believe in salvation by power in greater control. Either way – escape or power – anarchy is nothing more than a short cut to tyranny. Marxism used the disenchantment of some people to create so much chaos that the only solution to a nation's problems is totalitarian rule. Under communism, anarchy is the first ideology eliminated after the revolution succeeds.

Many Christians, who have grown frustrated at the slow progress God's people seem to be making in society, have turned to anarchy as the only solution to a creeping tyranny. Consider David's response to murderous King Saul. Did David murder Saul when Saul persecuted him? David was forced to flee Israel and pretend to be crazy in the presence of the Philistines – and not just the Philistines, but the king of Gath, the city of Goliath (1 Samuel 21:10-15). David was God's anointed, yet he did not challenge Saul, nor did he surrender. He wrote, "I shall not die, but live, and declare the works of the Lord" (Psalm 118:17).

Anarchy is the way of historical losers and short-sighted thinkers. It is not surprising to learn that when Lenin began to consolidate his power in Russia after the Russian Revolution, he deported the anarchists or had them shot. Yet they had supported revolutionary violence in the name of abolishing all political and State blueprints. They cast off the rule of godly law and received nothing but the violent and evil rule of a petty dictator.

Autocracy

Another way to solve the dilemma of political power is to consolidate it in one man, to create a messianic figure. An Autocrat is someone who is an independent ruler. His power (*kratos*) is self-derived (*auto*). He continues in power by his own decree and is backed by military might. An example of this kind of political structure is found in the book of Judges where the Israelites are harassed by the Midianites: "and the power of Midian prevailed against Israel. Because of Midian the sons of Israel made for themselves the dens which were in the mountains and the caves and the strongholds" (Judges 6:2).

Israel's "predicament" was the result of disobedience: "Then the sons of Israel did what was evil in the sight of the Lord; and the Lord gave them into the hands of Midian seven years" (Judges 6:1). Instead of turning to God in repentance, the people looked for *political* solutions to their "problems." The people were trusting in their man-made "tower" (Judges 8:9). Instead of putting their trust in God as their "Mighty Fortress" (Psalm 46), they chose the supposed power of man and man's puny fortresses. Gideon promised to "tear down this fortress," this idol of security and salvation (Judges 8:9 cf. v. 17).

After Gideon defeated the enemies of Israel, the people were ready to set up a centralized political regime: "The men said, 'Rule over us, both you and your son, also your son's son, for you have delivered us from the hand of Midian'" (Judges 8:22). The problem the Israelites had with the Midianites happened because they had rejected God as their King. Now that God had delivered them, they still failed to acknowledge that "The Lord should rule over them" (Judges 8:23). Instead, they opted for a centralized humanistic, and perpetual social order with Gideon and his family as permanent rulers. To them, Gideon was more than a judge, a localized civil ruler, he was to be their king who would sit on a throne and make them secure. A centralized social order seemed better to them than putting one's trust for safety and security in the Lord!

With forty years of peace behind them, the people had forgotten who brought them peace (cf. Deuteronomy 8). The people began to "play the harlot with the Baals, and made Baal-berith their god" (Judges 8:33). Once again, the rejection of God as their King led them to look to man and some sort of centralized social order. One of

Gideon's sons, Abimelech attempted to centralize power and authority and place all sovereignty in himself. Abimelech took advantage of the weakened commitment of the people to the Lord. If they were ready to worship a synthetic god (*Baal-berith* means "Baal of the Covenant" – a mixture of Baalism and the promises of the Covenant), then they might have been ready to rally around him for security, a synthetic king. (Abimelech's father was an Israelite, while his mother was a Canaanite.) To ensure his scheme to power, Abimelech killed off all his political competition: "He went to his father's house at Ophrah, and killed his brothers the sons of Jerubbaal, seventy men, on one stone" (Judges 9:5).

Jotham escaped the bloodbath at Ophrah and went to Mount Gerizim to warn the Israelites not to rally around a king who promised security and at the same time demanded unconditional loyalty. The result of such an alliance would be their destruction. Jotham warned them in a parable, "And the bramble said to the trees, 'If in truth you are anointing me [Abimelech] as king over you, come and take refuge in my shade [the promise of security]; but if not, may fire come out from the bramble and consume the cedars of Lebanon [the reality of tyranny]' " (Judges 9:15).

As with all centralized political regimes, judgment and ruin are inevitable. This centralized administration of Abimelech was made up of "worthless and reckless fellows" from Shechem (Judges 9:4). It was not long before the administration of this new autocratic ruler fell into ruin, and those who followed him became disenchanted:

> *God sent an evil spirit between Abimelech and the men of Shechem; and the men of Shechem dealt treacherously with Abimelech, in order that the violence done to the seventy sons of Jerubbaal might come, and their blood might be laid on Abimelech their brother, who killed them, and on the men of Shechem, who strengthened his hand to kill his brothers. And the men of Shechem set men in ambush against him on the tops of the mountains, and they robbed all who might pass by them along the road; and it was told to Abimelech (vv. 23-25).*

An autocratic government is inherently unstable. Assassination and political coups are always present when there are other ambitious men seeking the same power. The people are rarely safe. Each successive ruler often changes the rules and regulations at his own whim. The people have little if any input into the working of the government. There is no check on the king's power. Samuel Rutherford (1600-1661), in an attempt to counter the "divine right of kings" position, which was nothing more than autocratic government, wrote *Lex Rex: or The Law and the Prince* in 1644. Rutherford's position put even the king under God's Law. As would be expected, *Lex Rex* was outlawed in England and Scotland. Rutherford's view so jeopardized the "divine right of kings" mandate that he was condemned to death for his views. He died before he could be executed as a rebel of the autocratic state.

Oligarchy

The word "oligarchy" is derived from a Greek word meaning "rule (*archein*) by the few (*oligos*)." In our day, the Supreme Court acts as an oligarchy. The justices on the Court are considered the final court of appeal. The law is what they say it is. The court is a closed system. Nothing outside the Court, and nothing higher than the Court rules. While Congress can overrule the Supreme Court and even impeach justices who consistently rule contrary to the Constitution, it rarely, if ever, happens. These justices are then an oligarchy by default.

Power in the hands of men whose only check is their own "sense" of what they believe is right or wrong puts a nation at risk. "Power corrupts," said Lord Acton, "and absolute power corrupts absolutely." What happens when a small group of men pronounce that an unborn child is not protected by the Constitution, that this helpless little life has no rights, that his "mother" has the constitutional right to kill the baby at will? Nine men, an oligarchy, have done just that; they have sentenced more than 20 million unborn babies to death.

Democracy

Most Americans are under the impression that our nation is a democracy. To be sure, there are democratic elements in our constitutional system. The First Amendment to the Constitution states that, "The people" have the right "to petition the Government for a redress of grievances." The petition of the people is only as good as the character of the people. Keeping in mind the Biblical doctrine of the depravity of man, our constitutional framers steered clear of a democracy. Constitutional attorney John W. Whitehead writes: "It must be remembered that the term *democratic* appears neither in the Declaration of Independence nor in the Constitution. Actually, when the Constitution is analyzed in its original form, the document is found to be a serious attempt to establish a government mixed with democratic, aristocratic, and monarchial elements – a government of checks and balances."

A democracy places all power in the people. It's a government of the masses. (The word "of" is tricky. It can mean "by" or it can mean "over." Many bloody tyrannies of our day have been imposed over the people in the name of the people.) Democratic law is based on the will of the majority. If the whims and fancies of the people change, the law changes. In the *Federalist Papers* (which were popular newspaper articles written in defense of the ratification of the Constitution in 1787 and 1788 by Alexander Hamilton, James Madison, and John Jay), democracies were described as "spectacles of turbulence and contention." Democracies are "incompatible with personal security or the rights of property . . . In general [they] have been as short in their lives as they have been violent in their death."

Democracies degenerate into exploitation because some voters discover that they can vote themselves political and financial favors out of the public treasury. Those seeking power through majority rule always vote for the candidate promising the most benefits. The results are certain: democracies collapse because the public treasury is milked dry because of greater voter demand. A dictatorship normally follows.

Socialism

Socialism, along with its illegitimate son Communism, is popular around the world. Socialism appeals to man's desire to get something for nothing through the agency of an omnipotent central government. Under Socialism, the means of production is owned by the state. The state interferes in the everyday affairs of all the people, even in the transactions they make. The state determines what will be produced, how much of an item will be produced, how it will be produced, where it will be produced, by whom it will be produced, what it will sell for, how people will get the product, and how it will be used.

Under Socialism, the individual is given little incentive to invent, produce a better product, or to be more efficient so a product can be sold at a lower price and thus benefit all of society. The State determines everything. Socialism is rarely democratic; that is, the people have little to say about who gets elected to office to set socialistic policies. Like a democracy, socialists stay in power by the "promise." The voting public is always "promised" a share of the State's monies. From this, the rulers are able to purchase the votes they need to stay in power. When the people are dissatisfied with one Socialist leader, they will vote him out for another who promises to make his promises good. The bottom line is that the rulers prostitute themselves in order to maintain power.

Those who submit to Socialism are rewarded. "Those who do not submit,"as the English Fabian socialist George Bernard Shaw (1856-1950) so urbanely quipped,"will be mercifully put out of the way." All socialism begins with "interventionism," the gradual manipulation of the economy through governmental decree. Again, it's always with the promise that things will be better if the State steps in to "fix" things.

Summary

The first principle of Biblical government – church, civil government, family, and self-government – is that God is in charge. Government must begin with *self-government under God.* This is as true of civil government as for all other forms of government.

Humanism's denial of God's government means in practice that the individual's will is absorbed and denied by the will of the government. Public policy overrules any contradictory policy held by an individual, a church, a business, or a civil jurisdiction at the federal, State, county, or city level. When tyranny finally happens, when the government's will becomes the people's will, the citizenry look at the prevailing conditions and ask how could it have happened. Fingers are pointed all around, when in fact, the finger-pointing ought to begin with each of us. Citizens rarely get a government that is more virtuous than themselves.

A nation that denies God's government over the individual, the family, the church, and the state, will find itself enslaved to those who want to be master. The sad thing is that many of us are willing to let it happen. But even more disturbing, we want it to happen. Sinful men are often in the mood to shift their God-given duties and responsibilities to those in government who they think will provide something for nothing. Sadly, few people who relinquish their liberties in an effort to be "free" from their responsibilities find the peace and prosperity they seek.

The doors of tyranny are closing. Are we motivated to follow God through the opening, or will we forever find ourselves locked in the grip of the willing power merchants who will use us for their evil ends? The choice is ours.

The term "government" has many meanings today. Most people define it in solely political terms. Older dictionaries, especially Noah Webster's *American Dictionary of the English Language* (1828), define "government" with a multiplicity of meanings and referring to numerous jurisdictions. Older textbooks see government as beginning in the home, what we would call "family government."

Government in the singular, referring to the rule of Christ, belongs to God alone. The church is also a legitimate government with authority and power. God has established multiple governing authorities, one of which is *civil* government. These many authorities were not designed to compete but to cooperate. Multiple created authorities are patterned after the Divine One and Many, the Triune God. The One is not to be exalted over the Many. The Many are not to be exalted over the One. The many governments established by God are each placed over a domain designated by God in Scripture. Civil government is a God-ordained government that has a very limited jurisdiction that is designed to punish evil doers and promote the good.

In summary:

1. Rulers speak in the name of the god of the society.
2. Societies are therefore ruled either by the words of God or by the words of men.
3. A nation that forgets God is doomed in history.
4. God is the ultimate source of peace and prosperity.
5. To say that any human institution provides us with peace and prosperity is to make a god of that institution.
6. God judges institutions that rule in the name of any other god.
7. The words of man can be manipulated by men.
8. One source of political power in history has been the ability of rulers to redefine words.
9. A shift in meaning has taken place in the word "government," where the term only means civil government.
10. Noah Webster's 1828 dictionary defined all government as beginning with self-government.
11. The Bible teaches that human governments are plural.
12. In the Bible, "the" government (singular) refers only to the rule of Christ.
13. God is the model for all governments.
14. God is a Trinity: both One and Many.
15. Anti-Christian views of government destroy either the unity or diversity of society.

Questions on the Text

1. The United States faces what choice that King Herod also faced?
2. What is the Biblical covenant structure by which we should properly order our lives, personally or corporately?
3. Why are so many of our important laws and constitutions being re-interpreted, contrary to the original intent of the authors of these documents?
4. Describe how the older definitions of the term "government" differs from its present-day usage.
5. When the Bible speaks of "government" in the singular, what does it refer to? And who is the "model" for all types of government?
6. What are the three basic categories of authority that God has established for the proper ordering of society?
7. What should be ultimate in society, the one or the many? Should we have one monolithic authority or each person be an authority unto oneself?
8. What kind of political structures do anti-Christian civilizations recommend?
9. What is anarchy and what Biblical principle does it violate?
10. What is autocracy and what Biblical illustration is used to depict this form of government?
11. Give a present day example of an oligarchy.
12. Is our government a democracy? What are some of the pitfalls of this political system?
13. Explain the fundamental tenants of socialism, and how it affects personal freedom.
14. What is the first principle of Biblical government?
15. What is the end result of humanism's denial of God's government?
16. Describe the various jurisdictions of government, starting with the singular rule of Christ.

The Christian Origins of American Civil Government

Our nation began as a Christian nation. Our earliest forefathers believed the Bible when it said, "By me, kings reign, and rulers decree justice" (Proverbs 8:15). But it seems that the general public is being brainwashed to believe that our nation was founded on some neutral morality base. Secularism, we are told, has always ruled the day. Religion in general, and Christianity in particular, had little to do with the founding of these United States. Education, law, and politics were purposely "separated" from any religious affiliation. So the critics of our early Christian heritage want us to believe.

The present educational establishment, for example, wants to bury the past so our children have no way of comparing our Christian history with the secularists' vision of the future. A recent study of textbooks bears this out. Paul E. Vitz, professor of Psychology at New York University, spent months of careful analysis of 60 textbooks used in elementary schools across the country. The study was sponsored by the Department of Education. The texts were examined in terms of their references to religion, either directly or indirectly. "The most striking thing," Vitz determined, "is the total absence of any primary religious text about typical contemporary American religious life. In particular, there is not one text reference to characteristic Protestant religious life in these books." When religious life is depicted, the references are so diluted as to be meaningless. For example, in a Spanish-speaking neighborhood, "churches have places for dances and sports events." Religion is trivialized. In another textbook, a "Puritan" church is not described as a center of religious life but rather as a center for summer piano festivals. For the secularist, religion is evolutionary. There was a time when people were religious. But now that we've come of age, we no longer need religion. Religion, in effect, is a projection of man's primitive past. Modern man can do without the superstitions of religious belief. What used to be places of worship are now nothing more than entertainment centers.

The present educational establishment wants to bury the truth so our children have no way of comparing the past with the secularists' version of history and their aspirations for the future. This tactic eliminates discussion and conflict. It is time that our nation is reintroduced to the past. As Christians, we must not remain silent while nearly every vestige of Christianity is being removed from public life: from the gospel being denied in Public (government) schools to the removal of signs that the Salvation Army put on buses in Fresno, California that read: "God bless you."

A Christian Commonwealth

Both religious and political persecution motivated our forefathers to leave the shores of England and to start a "Christian Commonwealth" in the New World. The purpose of the New England colonies was, with respect to church and state, twofold: First, to establish the true and free church, free of the control of the state, free to be a

162

co-worker in terms of the Kingdom of God, to establish God's Zion on earth. Second, to establish godly magistrates, i.e., a Christian state, magistrates as ordained by God.

The separation of Christianity from the workings of the state was never in the minds of these early settlers. The following evidence will show that Christianity was the motivational force behind this nation's advance.

The history of this nation began, not in 1776, but more than a century earlier. Since ideas have consequences, we should expect to see the beliefs of previous generations influencing subsequent generations. It's true that even today, the influence of our Christian forefathers is making an impact, albeit a small one.

William Bradford (1589?-1657), in his *History of Plymouth Plantation*, wrote,

> *A great hope and inward zeal they had of laying some good foundation, or at least to make some way thereunto, for the propagating and advancing the Gospel of the Kingdom of Christ in those remote parts of the World; yea, though they should be but even as stepping stones unto others for the performing of so great a work.*

The Mayflower Compact, drafted prior to the Pilgrims' arrival off Cape Cod on November 11, 1620, was the first republican document of the New World, a forerunner to the United States Constitution. It reads in part:

> *In the name of God, Amen. We, whose names are underwritten, the loyal subjects of our dread sovereign lord King James, by the grace of God, ...having undertaken for the glory of God and advancement of the Christian faith, and the honor of our king and country, a voyage to plant the first colony in the northern parts of Virginia; do by these presents, solemnly and mutually in the presence of God and one another, covenant and combine ourselves together into a civil body politic, for our ordering and preservation and furtherance of other ends aforesaid...*

The First Charter of Virginia emphasizes the Christian character of the infant nation:

> *We, greatly commending and graciously accepting of their desires for the furtherance of so noble a work, which may by the providence of Almighty God hereafter tend to the glory of His Divine Majesty, in propagating of the Christian religion to such people, as yet live in darkness and miserable ignorance of the true knowledge and worship of God...*

The Fundamental Orders of Connecticut, drafted in January 14, 1639 at Hartford, was the first written constitution that created a civil government. It read in part:

> *Forasmuch as it has pleased the Almighty God by the wise disposition of His divine providence so to order and dispose [these]...lands...; and well knowing where a people are gathered together the Word of God requires that to maintain*

the peace and union of such a people there should be an orderly and decent government established according to God, to order and dispose of the affairs of all the people at all seasons as occasions shall require; do therefore associate and conjoin ourselves to be as one public State of Commonwealth, and do for ourselves and our successors and such as shall be adjoined to us at any time hereafter, enter into combination and confederation together, to maintain and preserve the liberty and purity of the Gospel of our Lord Jesus which we now profess, as also the discipline of the churches, which according to the truth of the said Gospel is now practiced among us...

The New England Confederation, put into effect on May 19, 1643, established a union of like-minded civil bodies:

Whereas we all came into these parts of America with one and the same end and aim, namely, to advance the Kingdom of our Lord Jesus Christ and to enjoy the liberties of the Gospel in purity with peace; and whereas in our settling (by a wise providence of God) we are further dispersed upon the sea coasts and rivers than was as first intended...

These early governmental documents have several things in common. First, they are not revolutionary documents, calling on men to overthrow the existing order through armed conflict. Second, God is acknowledged as the King and Sovereign, and earthly kings must bow in submission to His revealed will. Third, the adherents of these documents came to the New World to "advance the kingdom of the Lord Jesus Christ" and not some utopian, state-sponsored political order. Fourth, the Bible was accepted as the standard for an "orderly and decent government" as well as "for the discipline of churches." Fifth, the gospel preceded the advance of civilization. Sixth, the people covenanted with God before they "combined and confederated together." Seventh, their future depended upon faithfulness to God's commands. Eighth, liberty was the fruit of a Christian world order.

What About the Constitution?

On adoption of the U.S. Constitution in 1789, there was fear that the new national government would either interfere with the various States that had established religions (nine of the thirteen colonies) or institute a national church, making each State conform to the decree of Congress. Because of these fears, many States petitioned the First Congress to include a Constitutional Amendment prohibiting the national government from funding a single Christian denomination and favoring it with legal action. This is why, historically, "the real object of the [F]irst Amendment was not to countenance, much less to advance Mohammedanism [Islam], or Judaism, or infidelity, by prostrating Christianity, but to exclude all rivalry among Christian sects [denominations] and to prevent any national ecclesiastical establishment which would give to an hierarchy the exclusive patronage of the national government." Such was the opinion of Chief Justice Joseph Story in the mid-19th century.

When the First Amendment was drafted, nine of the thirteen States had established churches. The First Amendment was a guarantee to the States that the States would be able to continue whatever church-state relationship existed in 1791 (the year the Bill of Rights was ratified and made part of the Constitution). Maryland, North Carolina, South Carolina, and Georgia all shared Anglicanism as the established religion. Congregationalism was the established religion in Massachusetts, New Hampshire, and Connecticut. New York, while not having an established church, allowed for the establishment of Protestant religions. Only in Rhode Island and Virginia were all religious sects disestablished. But the Christian religion was the foundation of all the States. Their social, civil, and political institutions were based on the Bible. Not even Rhode Island and Virginia renounced Christianity, and both States continued to respect and acknowledge the Christian religion in their systems of law.

Congressman James Madison, the chief author of the First Amendment, informed his Congressional colleagues that he was responding to the desires of the various State Conventions to prohibit establishment of a national religion where one religious "sect might obtain a pre-eminence" over others.

As legal scholars point out, the critical word in the First Amendment's religion clauses is "respecting." "Congress shall make no law respecting an establishment . . . ," where "respecting" is synonymous with "concerning," "regarding," and "about." Professor Robert Cord writes that the provision does not "prohibit an establishment of religion; rather it prohibits Congress from making laws about, concerning or regarding an establishment of religion [i.e., the establishment of one denomination (sect) over all others]."

National Prayers

After passage of the First Amendment, the First Congress petitioned the President to proclaim a *national* day of prayer and thanksgiving. The issue was raised by Rep. Tucker that prayer "is a religious matter and, as such is proscribed to us. If a day of thanksgiving must take place, let it be done by the authority of the several states..." The prayer resolution passed in spite of the objections of Rep. Tucker and others. On September 25, 1789, the same day that it approved the First Amendment, Congress called on President Washington to proclaim a national day of prayer and thanksgiving. The First Congress resolved:

> *That a joint committee of both Houses be directed to wait upon the President of the United States to request that he would recommend to the people of the United States a day of public thanksgiving and prayer, to be observed by acknowledging, with grateful hearts, the many [notable] favors of Almighty God, especially by affording them an opportunity peaceably to establish a Constitution of government for their safety and happiness.*

The First Congress also established the Congressional chaplain system by which official daily prayers to God are still offered. In the entire debate on the First Amendment, not one word was said by any congressman about a "wall of separation between church and state" that would outlaw such a practice.

Government Buildings and Inscriptions

If men refuse to glorify God, He is able from stones to raise up children to praise Him (Matthew 3:9). The courts, through the legal maneuverings of the ACLU (which stands for the "American Civil Liberties Union"), are working to remove every vestige of Christianity from our land. Nevertheless, our Christian heritage is still etched in stone, in coins, on walls, on canvas, and in glass.

1. The Ten Commandments hang over the head of the Chief Justice of the Supreme Court.

2. In the House and Senate chambers appear the words, "In God We Trust."

3. In the Rotunda is the figure of the crucified Christ.

4. On the walls of the Capitol dome, these words appear: "The New Testament according to the Lord and Savior Jesus Christ."

5. On the Great Seal of the United States is inscribed the phrase *Annuit Coeptis,* "God has smiled on our undertaking."

6. Under the Seal is the phrase from Lincoln's Gettysburg address: "This nation under God."

7. President Eliot of Harvard chose Micah 6:8 for the wall of the nation's library: "He has showed thee, O man, what is good; and what doth God require of thee, but to do justly, and to love mercy, and to walk humbly with thy God."

8. The lawmaker's library quotes the Psalmist's acknowledgment of the beauty and order of creation: "The heavens declare the glory of God, and the firmament showeth His handiwork" (Psalm 19:1).

9. Engraved on the metal cap on the top of the Washington Monument are the words: "Praise be to God." Lining the walls of the stairwell are numerous Bible verses: "Search the Scriptures," "Holiness to the Lord," and "Train up a child in the way he should go, and when he is old he will not depart from it."

10. The crier who opens each session of the Supreme Court closes with the words, "God save the United States and the Honorable Court."

11. At the opposite end of the Lincoln memorial, words and phrases to Lincoln's Second Inaugural Address allude to "God," the "Bible," "providence," the "Almighty," and "divine attributes."

12. The plague in the Dirksen Office Building has the words "IN GOD WE TRUST" in bronze relief.

13.   In the Capitol Building a room was set aside by the Eighty-third Congress to be used exclusively for the private prayer and meditation of Members of Congress. In this specially designated room there is a stained-glass window showing George Washington kneeling in prayer. Behind Washington a prayer is etched: "Preserve me, O God, for in Thee do I put my trust" (Psalm 16:1). The two lower corners of the window each show the Holy Scriptures and an open book and a candle, signifying the light from God's law: "Thy Word is a lamp unto my feet and a light unto my path" (Psalm 119:105).

The question then arises: If so much of American political history is Christian, where did we get the idea of the separation of church and state? The answer is: from infidel politicians and minority churches that did not want to be taxed for the benefit of other churches.

Thomas Jefferson's Humanist Legacy

Ask almost any American if he believes in the separation of church and state, and he will tell you he does. Ask him why, and he may say that "it is in the Constitution." It *isn't* in the Constitution. It never was. It was in a letter from Thomas Jefferson to a group of Baptists.

Jefferson responded on January 1, 1802 to a group of Danbury Connecticut Baptists who called him an "infidel." There is no question that those Baptists had him labeled correctly. He was indeed an infidel. He did not believe in the divinity of Christ, nor did he believe in the Bible as the Word of God. He even put together a special version of the Bible, one without any miracles in it. But he did believe in one thing: getting re-elected. He knew that he was dead politically if Christians ever found out what his true beliefs were, for Christians were the overwhelming majority politically. So he covered his tracks. He hid behind a smoke screen of false concern over religious integrity and a free conscience.

This was a smart tactic. Baptists were not part of any State religious establishment. They resented the fact that they had to pay taxes that went to support State churches – a reasonable resentment in retrospect, but not a commonly shared opinion in 1802, anywhere on earth. So he appealed to their sense of injustice. He understood their fears. He wrote:

> *Believing with you that religion is a matter which lies solely between man and his God, that he owes account to none other for faith or his worship, that the legislative powers of government reach actions only, and not opinions, I contemplate with sovereign reverence that act of the whole American people which declared that their legislature should "make no law respecting an establishment of religion, or prohibiting the free exercise thereof," thus building a wall of separation between church and state.*

The "wall of separation" language appealed to what was then a small religious sect that was discriminated against, the Baptists. Fifty years later, they had become the dominant Protestant group numerically, as they remain today. Jefferson, the theological infidel, wanted nothing more than to get Christians out of his hair politically. So, in effect, he offered them a political deal: you get out of my hair politically, and I will get out of your hair ecclesiastically.

This deal was repeated again and again in U.S. history. It rested on a myth, the myth of neutrality. It rested on another myth as well, the myth of natural law. It also rested on the greatest political myth in modern history: the separation of God and state. The infidels spoke of the separation of *church* and state, but what they were after was the separation of God and state, the separation of God's law and state, and (if they could achieve it), the separation of Christians from government. They wanted the Christians to *disenfranchise* themselves voluntarily, and to achieve this, they invented a new slogan, the separation of church and state. It worked, too, especially after 1925 (in the media reaction to the famous Scopes "monkey trial" over the teaching of evolution in government-funded high schools) until about 1975 (the candidacy of Jimmy Carter).

Jefferson had no hand in the drafting of the Constitution or the Bill of Rights. He was in France at the time. Since when do phrases in letters of presidents substitute for Constitutional language? Our forefathers have done a great disservice in perpetuating the myth of the separation of church and state.

What the Supreme Court Says Isn't Necessarily Law

The U.S. Constitution established the limitations of the Supreme Court from the beginning, although for the past century, few legal scholars and virtually no politicians have acknowledged what the Founders wrote into the Constitution. If Congress is convinced that the Court is usurping jurisdiction that belongs to Congress, they can remove appellate jurisdiction from the Supreme Court (Art. III, Sec. 2). This was done in a case in 1869, *Ex parte McCardle.*

It is interesting that law professors in prestigious law schools teach their students that what the Supreme Court says is not "the law," that it is not final, and they encourage their students to try to get cases overturned that appear to be settled by Supreme Court precedent. But in public, they seldom admit this. "Yes, what the Court says is the law of the land," they tell television interviewers. Then they return to their classrooms and tell their students that the Supreme Court has only decided one case at one point in time, but it has not decided the law of the land.

Summary

Jefferson's legacy had its origins in the "Enlightenment" where Reason was crowned as god, natural law substituted for Biblical law, and neutrality became the new legal fiction. The Christian community was sucked into the vortex of this emerging mythical world view. But institutions built on myths are collapsing. The world views based on reason over revelation, natural law over Biblical law, and neutrality over the religious presuppositions (of Thomas Jefferson in politics, Horace Mann and John Dewey in education, and Oliver Wendell Holmes in law), are disintegrating.

So, the goal is to steadily recover our religious-historical roots, but without such medieval mistakes as government-financed churches and government-financed schools. We need to get back to the tradition that Jefferson abhorred (God and His word-law as supreme even over civil government), but without restoring what the Baptists fought against (State-financed churches).

The First Amendment was added to the Constitution to protect the Church from a national establishment of religion. There is an abundant amount of evidence supporting the claim that America's early history was based on Biblical principles. The phrase "the separation of church and state" comes from a letter written by Thomas Jefferson. Jefferson had nothing to do with the drafting of the First Amendment.

Recent courts and humanist politicians have illegitimately substituted Jefferson's anti-Constitutional phrase in place of the First Amendment. The Communists followed their lead. The Soviet Constitution maintained that the "church is . . .separated from the state." What the Constitution was clearly designed to prevent – the intrusion by Congress into state and local ecclesiastical affairs – recent interpreters of the Constitution have mandated in the name of the Constitution. Christians who have never learned the Christian history of the United States have ignorantly and complacently gone along with this deliberate rewriting of American judicial history. They still think the words "the separation of church and state" are in the Constitution. They were in the Constitution of the former Soviet Union.

The humanists in the United States are no more "neutral" religiously than the humanists in the Soviet Union were. In both cases, the national government is assumed to have divine rights: immunity from judicial appeal. Religiously "neutral" natural law theory cannot protect Christians in the United States from the inevitable loss of liberty that every non-Christian system of government inevitably produces. There is only one appeal that can assure men of liberty: an appeal to God and His authoritative Word.

Questions on the Text

1. Our nation began as a Christian nation, but what does the present educational establishment want us to believe?
2. What documented proof is there that the current educational establishment is burying any trace of our Christian heritage as a fledgling nation?
3. How do secularists view religion?
4. What motivated our forefathers to leave England and start a new way of life?
5. Did our nation begin in 1776? If not, when?
6. What was William Bradford's purpose in coming to the New World in the early 1600's?
7. What was the first republican document of the New World? And was it a Christian document?
8. What noble work was the First Charter of Virginia based upon?
9. Describe how the virtues of peace, liberty and purity are tied together in the Fundamental Orders of Connecticut, as well as the New England Confederation.

10. In your own words, describe the opinion of Chief Justice Joseph Story, who spoke out in the middle 1800's concerning "the real object of the First Amendment."

11. Which of the thirteen original States had established churches? Which States allowed all religious sects?

12. What ironic resolution was passed the same day the First Amendment was approved?

13. What remarkable system was established by which official daily prayers to God were to be offered?

14. What is the group called the American Civil Liberties Union, trying to eradicate?

15. List three of the ten inscriptions or depictions found on our government buildings which reflect our Christian heritage.

16. Is the concept of the separation of church and state found in a legal, binding document? If not, where is it found?

17. Describe Thomas Jefferson's religious beliefs, and how they motivated him to deceitfully play on the Danbury Baptists' sense of injustice to distort the First Amendment's original intent.

18. Is the Supreme Court the law of the land? If not, what is?

19. What is the emerging mythical world view by which the Christian community has been duped?

20. What then should be our goal?

How to Write to Public Officials

Tips for Writing to Your Congressman

The following hints on how to write a member of Congress were suggested by congressional sources and the League of Women Voters.

- Write to your own senators or representatives. Letters sent to other members will end up on the desk of members from your state.
- Write at the proper time, when a bill is being discussed in committee or on the floor.
- Use your own words and your own stationery. Avoid signing and sending a form or mimeographed letter.
- Don't be a pen pal. Don't try to instruct the representative or senator on every issue that comes up.
- Whenever possible, identify all bills by their number.
- If possible, include pertinent editorials from local papers.
- Be constructive. If a bill deals with a problem you admit exists but you believe the bill is the wrong approach, tell what you think is the right approach.
- If you have expert knowledge or wide experience in particular areas, share it with the member. But don't pretend to wield vast political influence.
- Write to the member when he does something of which you approve. A note of appreciation will make him remember you more favorably the next time.
- Feel free to write when you have a question or problem dealing with procedures of governmental departments.
- Be brief, write legibly, and be sure to use the proper form of address. Feminine forms of address should be substituted, when appropriate.

Correct Form for Letters to Public Officials

President
The President
The White House
Washington, D.C. 20500

Dear Mr. President:

Very respectfully yours,

Senator
Honorable _____
United State Senate
Washington, D.C. 20510

Dear Senator:

Sincerely yours,

Member of the Cabinet
Honorable _____
The Secretary of _____
Washington, D.C. 20520

Dear Mr. Secretary:

Sincerely yours,

Vice President
The Vice President
Old Executive Office Bldg.
17th St & Pennsylvania Av N W
Washington, D.C. 20510

Dear Mr. Vice President:

Sincerely yours,

Representative
Honorable _____
House of Representatives
Washington, D.C. 20515

Dear Mr. _____

Sincerely yours,

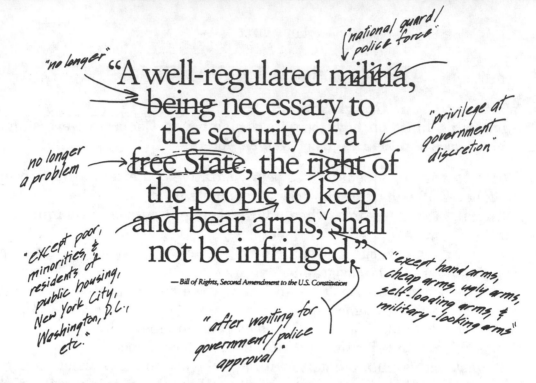

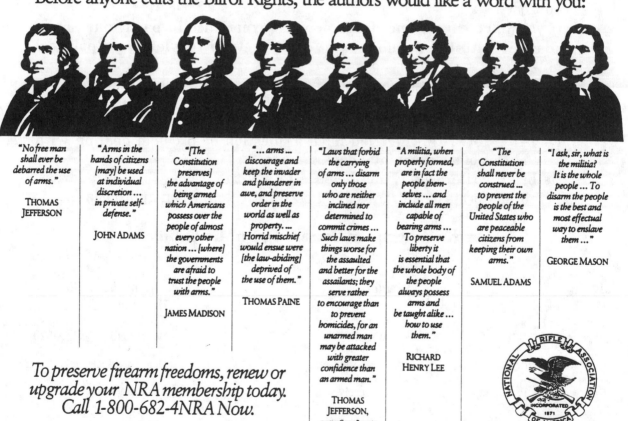

Political cartoons have been used to address important topics that are before the public eye since the days of Benjamin Franklin. The modern advertisement pictured above is a very good example of how effectively a "political statement" can be made by way of a simple cartoon.

HOW A BILL IS PASSED

A bill may originate in either the House or the Senate, and the procedure is almost identical. If it originates in the House:

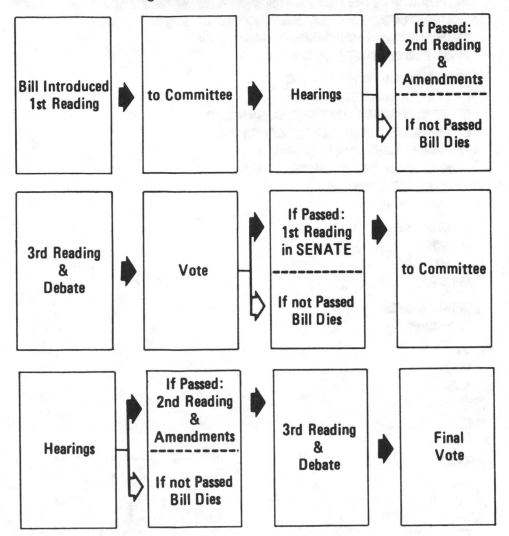

Each bill must be read by title on three different days in each house before it is passed. The first reading introduces the bill to the houses. The second reading allows for amendments of the bill. When a bill is called for its third reading, it is voted on for passage.

When the Senate does not amend an original House bill, the bill goes to the Governor for final action. The Governor may sign the bill, allow the bill to become law without his signature or veto the bill.

If the Senate amends the bill, it goes back to the House. If the House concurs with the Senate amendments, the bill goes to the Governor. The House may refuse to accept the Senate amendments, however. If the Senate withdraws its amendments, the bill goes to the Governor for his action. If the Senate will not withdraw its amendments, the bill goes to conference committee where differences may be worked out. If agreement is reached by both houses, the bill will go to the Governor for action.

If the amended bill is rejected by the House, and either the House or the Senate fails to approve the first conference committee report, the bill may go to a second conference committee. If either the House or the Senate does not approve the second conference committee report, the bill is dead.

FEDERAL BUDGET: Surpluses vs. Deficits (in billions by fiscal years)

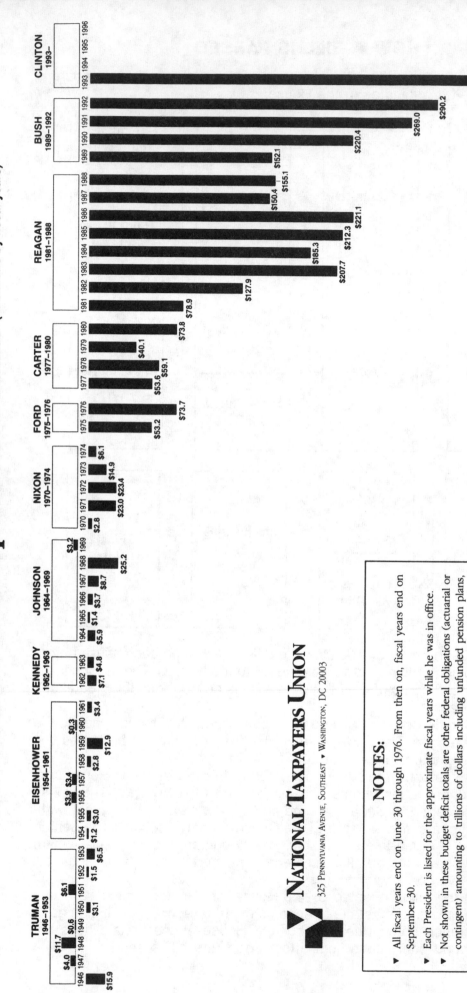

NATIONAL TAXPAYERS UNION

325 Pennsylvania Avenue, Southeast ▾ Washington, DC 20003

NOTES:

▸ All fiscal years end on June 30 through 1976. From then on, fiscal years end on September 30.

▸ Each President is listed for the approximate fiscal years while he was in office.

▸ Not shown in these budget deficit totals are other federal obligations (actuarial or contingent) amounting to trillions of dollars including unfunded pension plans, Social Security liabilities, loan and credit guarantees and other short and long-term commitments.

Sid Taylor, Research Director, February, 1993

INDEX